The

GREAT WORK

of the

GOSPEL

Claudio & Margarita —
May God continue to magnify
his grace in your life. You
love and support continue to be
part of God's grace in my life
Love you!

John ____
5-25-06

The GREAT WORK *of the* GOSPEL

HOW WE EXPERIENCE GOD'S GRACE

JOHN ENSOR

FOREWORD *by* JOHN PIPER

CROSSWAY BOOKS

A PUBLISHING MINISTRY OF
GOOD NEWS PUBLISHERS
WHEATON, ILLINOIS

The Great Work of the Gospel: How We Experience God's Grace

Copyright © 2006 by John Ensor

Published by Crossway Books
>   a publishing ministry of Good News Publishers
>   1300 Crescent Street
>   Wheaton, Illinois 60187

A revision of *Experiencing God's Forgiveness* (NavPress, 1997).

Cover design: Josh Dennis

Cover photo: Getty Images

First printing 2006

Printed in the United States of America

All emphases in Scripture citations have been added by the author.

Library of Congress Cataloging-in-Publication Data
Ensor, John M.
   The great work of the Gospel : how we experience God's grace /
John Ensor ; foreword by John Piper.
      p. cm.
   Includes bibliographical references (p.) and indexes.
   ISBN 13: 978-1-58134-773-9 (tpb)
   ISBN 10: 1-58134-773-1
   1. Grace (Theology).   I. Title
BT761.3.E57   2006
234—dc22   2005037845

VP		16	15	14	13	12	11	10	09	08	07	06
15	14	13	12	11	10	9	8	7	6	5	4	3	2	1

To friends from my youth—

the OLBERG family and the STODDA family,

*who by their kindness to me and their passion for God,
inspired an aimless teen to seek out
the Great Work of the Gospel above all else.*

CONTENTS

FOREWORD

I am a painfully slow reader. So I must be ruthless in the good things that I choose not to read. I did not begrudge the time it took to read the first edition of this book (then titled *Experiencing God's Forgiveness*). I started it because John Ensor is an admired friend. I finished it because it is a very good book. And now I welcome this gospel-centered revision. I expect that what I wrote of the earlier book will be true of this one as well.

I love the God-centeredness of this book. At one point I wrote in the margin, "John's great strength is reasserting the greatness of God in a way so compelling that God-neglecting moderns might feel it." In another place I wrote, "This book is a celebration of the greatness of Christ's work on the cross." And the cross is not the measure of our worth, but of God's. Christ's death for us is grounded firmly on "the value [God] places on himself and his own glory as a loving God." The book is a God-entranced vision of glorious forgiveness. "For your name's sake, O LORD, pardon my guilt" (Psalm 25:11).

The book succeeds because *it is biblical*. It is saturated with the Bible. John has a sweeping knowledge of Scripture and interprets it carefully. He would agree that the sieve of human thought is God's thought. So he says, "Only a truth-soaked mind can reshape our opinions, attitudes, responses, and decisions." It is a vibrantly truth-driven book.

It also succeeds because *it is real*. It connects with life. John writes with the savvy of one who has seen the legal and justice system from the inside. He has struggled with the most impossible crises. He has lost friends in murder. He has gained friends from converted criminals. He knows the street. He has learned some deep things; "If I come across a man raping a woman, I cannot love both of them in the same way." His God-centeredness grew in abortion wars and drug deals and manifold cases of abuse. What you read here has been tested in fire.

The book succeeds because *it is full of compassion and hope*. The glory of God is mainly the glory of his mercy. And the way to make it known is to move from guilt to gladness by faith. Under God the persons that count most are the broken, trapped, hopeless sinners. "God desires to make his *mercy* the apex of his own glory in the eyes of all creation. It is the ultimate reason for the creation of the world and the plan of redemption."

But for all its emphasis on compassion, *the book is not sappy.* John is Jesus-like in his utter freedom from sentimentality. He is, in fact, strikingly blunt. "Murmuring is God-hatred in the acorn stage." Our deepest problem is not our "woundedness" but our "wayward-ness." There is such a thing as "healthy shame." The wrath of God is "terrible . . . fierce . . . awful." One thing God will not forgive is the "discounting of the Great Work of grace wrought by the Spirit."

Yet for all its bluntness *it is a happy book.* "To believe means to trust that God's outworking plan will in the end lead to [our] joy and his glory." "The faith we are to place in God is a glad willingness to trust that he will provide for us everything that will truly make us happy in the long run." John is gripped by the great truth that God is most glorified in us when we are most satisfied in him.

The Great Work of the Gospel is God-centered good news. It is the kind of message that will make deep, strong people and deep, strong churches. It will release people from the self-absorbed ratio-nalizations that keep us from the fullest engagement in the global cause of God. So I am hopeful that for God's sake the gladness on the other side of guilt will also be the gladness of the nations—in God.

—John Piper
Bethlehem Baptist Church
Minneapolis, Minnesota
December 7, 2005

INTRODUCTION

The Human Experience of God's Outworking Grace

Grace is but glory begun, and glory is but grace perfected.
—JONATHAN EDWARDS

Now to him who is able to do far more abundantly than all that we ask or think, according to the power at work within us, to him be glory.
—EPHESIANS 3:20-21A

Alexander Pope's famous axiom, "To err is human, to forgive, divine,"[1] points to the theme of this book. It is about our *human experience* of God's outworking *grace*—the sin-forgiving gift of it, the guilt-removing power of it, the soul-satisfying joy of it, the cross-suffering mystery of it, the conscience-cleansing experience of it, the life-transforming quality of it, the muscular faith-building impact of it, the eternally reconciling splendor of it.

Understanding how God works this out and seeing how we experience his grace as human beings is what I am after. It is his Great Work.

I say this for three reasons.

1. *Because the problem is the greatest of all problems.* "The problem of forgiveness," wrote John Stott, "is constituted by the inevitable collision between divine perfection and human rebellion; between God as he is and us as we are."[2] What is becoming more self-evident to me, the longer I live, is the deep-seated and pervasive nature of human sinfulness. During the early years of the twentieth century, there was much glib talk of man evolving into a higher level of moral development. The First World War challenged the notion. The Second, reaching the apex of human depravity in the Holocaust, shattered the idea. Today's terrorism stuns us only as to the *depth* of human hatred and cruelty.

Jesus said, "he who is forgiven little, loves little" (Luke 7:47). If I have only a little problem with sin, I need only a little favor. The faith that turned the world upside down, however, was an *amazing grace*.

Forgiveness is God's Great Work for another reason:

2. *Because the solution is the most excellent of all solutions.* The cross is the greatest surprise of human history. None of the religions of the world could even have thought of such a thing. Indeed even the closest associates of Christ never saw it coming. None understood *the plan* of it. When one discovers the reason for it and the wisdom of it and the nature of it, one understands why Christianity is "Christ crucified" (1 Corinthians 1:23). It is not simply a code of ethics or a set of principles for wise living, like those provided by Benjamin Franklin or Confucius. It is God at work in human life through the cross.

The unique character of Christianity as a religion of *music* is evidence for this excellence. The cross inspires song. No other religion inspires such a burning passion to put words of praise to music. Hymns, gospel songs, oratorios, choruses pour out of the cross in every language and in every ethnomusicological form in a never ending stream. Take the cross out of the mountain of music and you have a molehill. Such is the wonder of God's solution to our sin.

The third reason to call God's work of grace his Great Work is:

3. *Because the change it produces is the most extreme change possible.* God's grace takes a thief and convicts him. It not only forgives him for stealing but makes him abhor any thought of ever stealing again. Then it prompts him to make restitution and to find honest work to meet his needs. Then it gives him a heart to work harder and earn more, so that he might have something to give to charity. The apostle Paul says, "Let the thief *no longer steal,* but rather *let him labor,* doing honest work with his own hands, so that he may have something to *share* with anyone in need" (Ephesians 4:28). This is the

change that God does in the work of grace; he turns a thief into a philanthropist.

I have a good friend who is a doctor. Just a few years ago he was an abortionist for Planned Parenthood. He exploited the fears of pregnant women and profited in the shedding of innocent blood. Today he works beside me in running a pregnancy help ministry. He offers his medical services *free of charge* and has *spent* large amounts of money to purchase ultrasound equipment so that women might understand their decision more clearly. What accounts for such a transformed life? What explains such a contrasting before and after? God's grace, in all its *ongoing and outworking power.*

The grace of God that forgives us changes us. It changes us not just initially but continually as well. It convicts us and troubles our conscience. Later on it comforts us, "wiping away every tear" (see Revelation 21:4). Soon after, it unleashes irrepressible shouts of praise. The grace of God wounds our pride but then increases our confidence. When God forgives, he exposes the most shameful things only to then cleanse them all from our conscience. And that is just the *early* work of God in the outworking of his grace.

In the ongoing outworking of God's grace, God reorients our passions. "The grace of God has appeared, bringing *salvation* for all people, *training* us to renounce ungodliness and worldly passions" (Titus 2:11-12). It produces a radical joy and a strong faith, one that can endure great suffering and yet trust that, in the end, God's plan will lead to our joy and his glory. The grace that turns us from evil makes us "eager to do what is good" (Titus 2:14, NIV). The American theologian and philosopher Jonathan Edwards (1703–1758) said, "Grace is but glory begun, and glory is but grace perfected."[3] I want to trace out how this is true and track the human experience of grace doing this perfecting and glorifying work.

WHY DO I CALL IT "OUTWORKING GRACE"?

I call it "outworking grace" to get away from the more static idea of grace being a singular event, such as going to the movie theater or graduating from college. People get the idea that biblical grace means

largely the event of being forgiven. What happens after is either sec-
ondary or extra or supplementary. By outworking grace I mean what
Christ meant when he commissioned Paul to the gospel ministry: "I
am sending you to *open* their eyes, so that they may *turn* from darkness to light and from the power of Satan to God, that they may
receive forgiveness of sins and a place among those who are *sanctified*
by faith in me" (Acts 26:17-18). The work of grace here consists of
opening eyes *and* turning hearts *and* receiving forgiveness *and* being
sanctified. It is all *one* work of grace but it works itself out in terms
of our human experience, in an ongoing, life-changing dynamic.

By outworking grace I am after what Philippians 2:12-13 calls us
to go after: "*Work out* your own salvation with fear and trembling,
for it is *God who works in you,* both to will and to work for his good
pleasure." What is it that *we* are to work out with fear and trembling?
And how is *God* at work in us producing these changes? What comes
with salvation that needs to be worked out into our minds, our
tongues, our wallets, and our sex lives? How is it that when my sins
are forgiven, my neighborhood is improved?

In terms of human experience, in fear and trembling, we face the
responsibility to repent: "*Repent* therefore, and turn again, that your
sins may be blotted out, that times of refreshing may come" (Acts
3:19-20). Yet repentance is the work of God. Paul instructed Timothy
to teach patiently, saying, "God may perhaps *grant them repentance*
leading to a knowledge of the truth" (2 Timothy 2:25).

We are commanded to believe: "*Believe* in the Lord Jesus, and you
will be saved" (Acts 16:31). As a human experience, this comes down
to a decision of the will. But God is at work in our willing: "For it has
been *granted* to you that for the sake of Christ you should not only
believe in him but also suffer for his sake" (Philippians 1:29).

In fear and trembling, we are to keep God's commandments: "by
this we know that we have come to know him, if we *keep* his commandments" (1 John 2:3). But this is God at work: "And I will put
my Spirit within you, and *cause* you to walk in my statutes and be
careful to obey my rules" (Ezekiel 36:27).

In working out our salvation we are to set our hearts and minds
after God: "Set your minds on things that are above, not on things

that are on earth" (Colossians 3:2). But God is at work when it comes to our hearts and minds. So we find Paul praying "that the God of our Lord Jesus Christ, the Father of glory, may *give* you a spirit of wisdom and of revelation in the *knowledge* of him, having the eyes of your hearts *enlightened,* that you may know what is the hope to which he has called you" (Ephesians 1:17-18).

We are to live to God: "I urge you to live a life worthy of the calling you have received" (Ephesians 4:1, NIV). And yet, "you, who were dead in your trespasses . . . God *made* alive" (Colossians 2:13). In terms of human experience we must "be *strong* in the Lord" (Ephesians 6:10). But because it is God at work, Paul says, "May you be *strengthened* with all power, according to his glorious might, for all endurance and patience with joy" (Colossians 1:11). It is ours as a human experience to "rejoice in the Lord" (Philippians 4:4). Yet even in this, God is at work in us! "For you, O LORD, have *made* me glad by your work" (Psalm 92:4). We are to take heed and be careful, lest we fall (1 Corinthians 10:12). But it is God "who is able to *keep* you from stumbling" (Jude 24). We may indeed "serve the Lord" (Romans 12:11), but our honest testimony will be similar to Paul's human experience: "I was *made* a minister according to the gift of God's grace, which was given me by *the working of his power*" (Ephesians 3:7). And we could go on. It is *our* experience of *God's* outworking grace.

But it is not a partnership. It is not "I do half and God does half." It is God's work. Instead of a picture in our mind of meeting God halfway, a better picture might be that of dead Lazarus. Jesus called out for Lazarus to rise up (John 11:43), but with the call came the powerful work of grace, as Jesus raised Lazarus from the dead. Without that enabling power, Lazarus would not even have heard the call, let alone heeded it.

THE OUTWORKING OF GOD'S GRACE IN THE LIFE OF DAVID

Michelangelo's statue of David shows him as the archetypal man—rugged and handsome, courageous, visionary, manly in form and temperament. The real David is more pocked and cracked. Scripture does affirm that he was a man after God's own heart (see 1 Samuel 13:14; Acts 13:22). But he was also like Woody Allen, who said, "The heart wants what the heart wants."

This was David's condition when we pick up his story in 2 Samuel 11. It was in the spring of the year, when kings lead their armies into battle. But King David was at home. Already in the wrong place, he was vulnerable. Henri Nouwen quotes the rabbinical proverb, "He who thinks that he is finished is finished."[4] First Corinthians 10:12 (NIV) says it this way: "So, if you think you are standing firm, be careful that you don't fall!"

David was on the roof of his house, killing time, when he spotted Bathsheba bathing nude across the way. She was a very beautiful woman (2 Samuel 11:2) and David wanted her.

Bathsheba's husband, Uriah, was at this time away on the battlefield, risking his life in the service of king and country. David betrayed Uriah's service and used his own name and position to seduce Bathsheba. Soon after, he learned that Bathsheba was pregnant.

In an effort to hide his actions, David ordered Uriah home under the guise of needing a war report. He then granted Uriah liberty to go home to his wife before returning to battle.

David's plan, of course, was that Uriah would sleep with his wife and be deceived into thinking that Bathsheba's baby was theirs. But Uriah was a man of honor. He thought it dishonorable to enjoy the pleasures of marital intimacy when his brothers were away from their families, fighting and dying. He slept on the palace porch that night.

King David increased the pressure. He delayed Uriah's return to battle another night and insisted he eat and drink with him. He got Uriah drunk in an effort to loosen his code of honor. That too failed. Uriah again slept on the porch. But David would have his way. He sent Uriah back to battle with a note for his general that read, "Set Uriah in the forefront of the hardest fighting, and draw back from him, that he may be struck down, and die" (2 Samuel 11:15).

David, just by being home rather than with his army, was guilty of abandoning his responsibility as commander in chief. That by itself is no small sin, as any soldier will tell you. To this sin he added the sin of lust and the abuse of power. Then the cover-up began. He deceived and manipulated. He rewarded a soldier's deep devotion with the ultimate betrayal. He murdered him. As if nothing were wrong, perhaps even to look merciful, David took Bathsheba into his house as a wife and pretended that everything was just fine.

But God, who, we might say, was a God after David's own heart, now moved to deal with David's sin. He sent Nathan the prophet to confront David:

> "Thus says the LORD, the God of Israel, 'I anointed you king over Israel.... And I gave you your master's house and your master's wives into your arms and gave you the house of Israel and of Judah. And if this were too little, I would add to you as much more. Why have you despised the word of the LORD, to do what is evil in his sight? You have struck down Uriah the Hittite with the sword and have taken his wife to be your wife and have killed him with the sword of the Ammonites. Now therefore the sword shall never depart from your house, because you have despised me and have taken the wife of Uriah the Hittite to be your wife'" (2 Samuel 12:7-10).

I see in this devastating indictment the profound and life-changing work of God's forgiveness as it is designed for David's life. Why do I say this? Because by the time all is said and done in this affair, Nathan will add, "The LORD also has put away your sin; you shall not die" (12:13).

God's forgiveness was at work here. Nathan's message to David was "a severe mercy."[5] Nathan's probing ("Why did you despise the word of the LORD by doing what is evil in his eyes?") and indicting ("You struck down Uriah the Hittite with the sword and took his wife to be your own") and reasoning ("And if all this had been too little, I would have given you even more") forced David to consider his life before God (as we will discuss in chapter 1). David's denial broke: "I have sinned against the LORD" (12:13). This is the prerequisite work of grace. We must own up to our real guilt (chapter 2). David wept and fasted before the Lord (12:21). David discovered what the old preachers called "the exceeding sinfulness of sin" and acknowledged the justice of God's judgment (chapter 3). He cried,

> For I know my transgressions,
>   and my sin is ever before me.
> Against you, you only, have I sinned
>   and done what is evil in your sight,
> so that you may be justified in your words
>   and *blameless* in your judgment (Psalm 51:3-4).

The ongoing outworking of God's grace taught David that the consequences of sin outweigh the "fleeting pleasures" of sin. There was loss, though not eternal loss. As for the temporal consequences for David: "Behold, I will raise up evil against you out of your own house. And I will take your wives before your eyes and give them to your neighbor, and he shall lie with your wives in the sight of this sun. For you did it secretly, but I will do this thing before all Israel and before the sun'" (2 Samuel 12:11-12). In the subsequent years of his life, David witnessed sexual immorality, betrayal, murder, and death among his own family members (2 Samuel 11–21), just as he had done these things secretly against the household of Uriah. But, although there were serious and painful consequences for David's sin, as there is with ours, Nathan reassured David, "The LORD also has put away your sin; you shall not die" (12:13).

From this David learned to ask for forgiveness and to put his hope in God (chapter 4):

> Have mercy on me, O God,
>   according to your steadfast love;
> according to your abundant mercy
>   blot out my transgressions.
> Wash me thoroughly from my iniquity,
>   and cleanse me from my sin! (Psalm 51:1-2).

How God would answer this prayer (chapter 5) or justify it (chapter 6) was unclear to David. But this did not stop David from seeking a cleansed conscience (chapter 7):

> Purge me with hyssop, and I shall be clean;
> wash me, and I shall be whiter than snow (51:7).

And still God's grace is not finished. David anticipated that grace would relieve his burden and gladden his heart (chapter 8):

> . . . let the bones that you have broken rejoice.
> Hide your face from my sins,
> and blot out all my iniquities (51:8b-9).

He prayed for more grace, for a stronger and better relationship with God marked by praise and persevering faithfulness:

> Restore to me the joy of your salvation,
> and uphold me with a willing spirit (51:12).

This is what I mean by the outworking of God's grace. This is why I have concluded that it is God's Great Work and can say with David,

> Bless the Lord, O my soul,
> and forget not all his benefits—
> who *forgives* all your iniquity,
> and heals all your diseases,
> who redeems your life from *the pit,*
> and crowns you with steadfast love and mercy,
> who *satisfies* you with good
> so that your youth is *renewed* like the eagle's (Psalm 103:2-5).

Here is a "my-life-is-in-the-pits" rescuing work. Here is forgiveness for all my sins. Here is a crowning life-achievement award. Here is the heart made glad with goodness. Here is youth-like renewing strength in God. That's the human experience of God's outworking grace that I am after.

THE GREAT WORK OF THE GOSPEL

GROUP STUDY QUESTIONS

1. In this book, "the Great Work" refers to the great work of the *gospel*. Summarize why we are calling it the Great Work.

2. In your life to date, how have you perceived God at work in your life?

3. We have seen how much change can occur in our lives through the Great Work, turning thieves into philanthropists, for example, or turning a persecutor such as Paul into a passionate proclaimer of the gospel. Whom have you seen changed by the outworking of God's grace, and how?

4. In Philippians 2:12-13, Paul calls us to "work out our salvation with fear and trembling." He also calls us to see "God at work" in us when we take human initiative. This is a difficult concept to grasp. How does the raising of Lazarus help us grasp the concept? In what ways have we seen the need for human initiative in pursuing God and yet have seen that this is God at work?

1

THE GREAT WORK CONSIDERED

Asking Life-Changing Questions

Is there in the whole world a person who would have the right to forgive and could forgive?

—FYODOR DOSTOYEVSKY

For I delivered to you as of first importance what I also received: that Christ died for our sins

—1 CORINTHIANS 15:3

In searching out the grace of God according to the Bible, it does not take long to be surprised. The apostle Paul said, "For I delivered to you as of *first importance* what I also received: that Christ died for our sins" (1 Corinthians 15:3). A matter of first importance? The top priority in life? I once had the disturbing experience of being told, "I forgive you." It was disturbing because I had not asked for it. I was not looking for it and I did not sense that I needed it. In terms of our human experience, the gospel seems to do the same thing. It seeks to scratch where we feel no itch. It offers as a matter of first importance what we consider of least concern—God's forgiveness, reconciliation, and new life through the life and work of Jesus Christ.

Nonetheless, there it is. It is something to consider.

BILLY'S FEAR

Billy is a "personal trainer," the guy assigned to me at my local gym to show me how to use the various weight machines safely and effectively. He is a young, handsome, unmarried man of about thirty. He appears to be hard-working, college educated, and a decent fellow.

He interrupted my grunting on the weight machine one day, asking, "So you're a minister, right?"

I nodded yes.

"And that means I could ask you a question about God?"

I nodded again.

He looked around as if he were about to tell me where he hid the gold and whispered, "Do you think God is upset by some of the things we do?"

I was taken aback. I rarely find people in our contemporary culture openly wrestling with such grave spiritual concerns.

"Yes, I do," I replied. "In fact I think God is *angry* over some of the things we do."

It was Billy's turn to look surprised. He clearly was hoping I would assuage his feeling of guilt, not confirm it. "I'm worried about that," he said.

We were interrupted at that moment by someone who needed help on the cross trainer, and I was left alone with my flabby abs to wonder about the state of Billy's soul. His conscience was troubled. He sensed that all was not well between him and God. The matter of forgiveness was becoming a matter of *importance* to him. He was starting to wonder out loud, "How can I get right with God? Is it too late? How do I get my sins forgiven?" These are basic questions. I admit that they are jarringly out of tune with modern sensibilities. But maybe they are simply questions we do not ask *out loud* because of modern sensibilities.

ALICE'S DESPAIR

Alice was a college student who was raised in a strict Christian home. I was manning a pregnancy distress hotline when she called. She was so scared that even after we talked for an hour, she was still too afraid to tell me her first name. "Call me X," she said.

Alice had fallen into a sexual relationship for the first time. Physically and emotionally sickened with feelings of guilt, she left school. Since she had no place to go, she stayed with her boyfriend. She was also terrified that she might be pregnant. The shame that an out-of-wedlock pregnancy would bring to her family was paralyzing. The thought of an abortion, which she believed was murder, terrorized her further. In this desperate act of self-preservation, she thought, God would despise her as she despised herself.

Alice asked me, "Are you a Christian?"

"Yes," I answered.

"I *used* to be a Christian," she replied, "but I lost my salvation."

"Interesting. Just how did you do that?" I asked.

Alice explained what I already knew. By "I lost my salvation," she meant that she had lost hope that she could, or even should, be forgiven by God. What she had done was so wrong, so unacceptable in her own mind, that it must surely be unacceptable to God. Therefore *she* was unacceptable. She was beyond the reach of God's forgiveness, or so she thought. If God is justified in condemning us, how can he justifiably forgive us?

ANTOINETTE'S PRESUMPTION

Antoinette's approach to the matter of grace and forgiveness was different still. She and her boyfriend, Rich, had lived together for nine years, since age sixteen. They had several children and now another baby was on the way. Rich needed help finding a job. They also wanted to get married. They came to me for help, and I was glad to help them.

Some weeks later, Antoinette called. "Pray for me," she said, "and ask God to forgive me for what I am about to do tomorrow." She was scheduled to terminate her nineteen-week, preborn child in the morning. She had lost her job. Rich could not find a second one, and she had grown afraid and depressed.

What could I say? To pray for permission to destroy an innocent life is to make a mockery of the entire Christian faith; it shows contempt for the grace of God and turns it into a license to do evil. Antoinette was dangerously confused about God's forgiveness. But many of us are.

Under these terms forgiveness is not extended—in fact, I think it angers God that we should even ask. It is like someone asking me for permission to rape my daughter. The very question ignites a holy rage in defense of my daughter and against her would-be assailant.

It is possible to be presumptuous when it comes to the matter of God's grace. The French cynic says, "The good God will forgive me; that is his job."[1] But is this true? Could this not be an example of "believing in vain" (1 Corinthians 15:2)? Is it possible to believe in the forgiveness of sins in an unacceptable manner?

EVA'S WOUND

Eva was a street-wise girl who grew up in poverty in the inner city. She had a rough edge to her that I liked immediately. I invited her to help on some volunteer project now long forgotten. But I will never forget her. The subject of our families came up. I was rambling on about how my wife and I were planning a birthday party for my daughter later that week. Eva shook her head.

"You want to hear about my family?" she asked. "I was ten years old when I started to smoke pot. When I was eleven I did this with my father. He bought me a line of cocaine when I was seventeen. That pretty much explains where I'm coming from."

I almost burst out in tears. What kind of father buys cocaine for his teenaged daughter? What kind of evil is this that robs a young girl of fatherly love and treats her to the perverse pleasures of snorting cocaine? Eva had spent years on the streets: drugs; alcohol; sexual promiscuity; and reaping the pain and anger that resulted. I went home and hugged my daughter that night. I felt angry at Eva's father, a man I had never met. How ought God to deal with him? Here forgiveness seems immoral, and surely a just God would not give it. But is it sinful of me to think so? Are my sins less sinful? And just how does the grace of God work itself out in Eva, so that she can forgive her father? Or should she?

ASKING THE LIFE-CHANGING QUESTIONS

In one of his great novels, Fyodor Dostoyevsky asked, "Is there in the whole world a person who would have the right to forgive and could forgive?"[2] There are *many* probing questions we can ask in our desire to get hold of a biblically based, God-glorifying, heartfelt experience of God's grace. Does God forgive? Does he forgive everyone or only some? Are there degrees of sin? Is speeding to church as bad as adultery? Is slander the same as slitting a throat? Does the forgiveness of God go only so far?

Aren't some things unforgivable? If righteousness demands that judges never condemn the innocent or acquit the guilty, how can God forgive the guilty? How can he wink at wickedness? Do rapists and murderers sit down in heaven with raped and murdered men, women, and children and say, "Let's all live in harmony"? Is that heaven? Isn't there hell to pay for our sins? And if there is, how can *I* ever escape it?

Will God be more willing to forgive me if I make a sincere effort to reform myself? Will it help if I punish myself in certain ways? How *can* God forgive me for what I've done? I condemn myself; how can God do less?

Why is the cross necessary? If God requires us to forgive others without requiring of them anything so drastic as a blood sacrifice, why doesn't God practice what he preaches and merely forgive? What happened on the cross? Why did Jesus go through with it? Can I have any assurance that God has forgiven me? What are the grounds for this assurance? Can I ever live without the painful shame of the past?

There comes a time in our lives when we want to know God's grace. Human experience—the experience of people doing wrong and being wronged—leads us to this place. We want to know God's grace as a heartfelt experience. We want to know it intellectually, meaning something our mind can see and rejoice in. We want to know that it's based on a higher authority than our own opinion, and we want to know how we ought to live in light of the experience.

GOD'S WINSOME INVITATION

A woman once came to see me about her unhappy marriage. Her husband was emotionally absent and inattentive, among other things. The marriage was in deep trouble, and she was looking for my help to save it—or so I thought. I met with her husband. We talked about his life, his goals, his marriage, and his children. We talked about his priorities in life and how his marriage was crumbling around him as he puttered around in his various hobbies. In the weeks that followed he looked at his failures as a husband and father and began to seek help and guidance. Changes soon appeared, welcome changes. Then the wife came to me, upset. She acknowledged the improvements but then told me she really did not expect it and she did not want him to change. She wanted out. I discovered that she had "left" the marriage a long time earlier. His repentance was too late.

Might this be analogous to our relationship with God? Is it too late to change and expect God to welcome our repentance? There are several reasons to believe not only that it is not too late but that God's grace is set to a hair-trigger. One reason we might be able to reach this conclusion is God's winsome invitation. He says in Isaiah 1:18,

> "Come now, let us *reason* together,
>   says the LORD:
> though your sins are like scarlet,
>   they shall be as white as snow;
> though they are red like crimson,
>   they shall become like wool."

What an amazing invitation: "Come now, let us *reason* together." The idea contains the notion of debate. God has anticipated our questions concerning our guilt, his justice, his love, and our desire to be happy. Here a gauntlet is thrown down. God is ready to contend with our mind, grapple for our heart, reconcile us to himself through a deep and cleansing process—turning blood-red stains into pure white joy. Here is an invitation to know and experience the grace of God. And there are others:

> "Come, everyone who thirsts,
>   come to the waters;
> and he who has no money,
>   come, buy and eat!

Come, buy wine and milk
without money and without price.
Why do you spend your money for that which is not bread,
and your labor for that which does not satisfy?
Listen diligently to me, and eat what is good,
and delight yourselves in rich food.
Incline your ear, and come to me;
hear, that your soul may live;
and I will make with you an everlasting covenant"
(Isaiah 55:1-3).

GOD'S BOLD PROMISE

Besides his winsome invitation, God has boldly promised to do a great work of grace. We read in Jeremiah 31:13, 33-34:

"Then shall the young women rejoice in the dance,
and the young men and the old shall be merry.
I will turn their mourning into joy;
I will comfort them, and give them gladness for sorrow. . . . "

"But this is the covenant that I will make . . . declares the LORD: I will put my law within them, and I will write it on their hearts. And I will be their God, and they shall be my people. . . . *For I will forgive their iniquity,* and I will remember their sin no more."

Here God declares his intention to do a great work of grace. He promises to turn our mourning into gladness. He promises to alter our thinking and our passions so that we delight in his laws (rather than discount them). "I will be their God" means he will reconcile us and unite us to him and his purposes. But note that all of this flows as part of the ongoing outworking of God's grace. *"For,"* he says, "I will *forgive* their iniquity, and I will *remember their sin no more."*

GOD'S DEEP MOTIVATION

There is one question that rises above all others, one question I did not think to ask until I was in seminary and took a course on the writings of Jonathan Edwards. Edwards, an eighteenth-century Puritan preacher and philosopher, has been called America's greatest thinker. He wrote a treatise titled *The End for Which God Created the World* (published 1765).[3] It asks why God does what he does. What motivates God to do one thing and not another? The reason this is important is that it gets to the very heart of the issue before us. What motivates God to want to forgive?

The fuller answer will develop as we go, but for now, let me summarize what I think the answer is. Why should we take God's invitation and promise to heart? Because God's own great passion is to glorify himself in our knowing him and enjoying him. More particularly, he wants to show us his grace; more particularly still, he wants to show us his infinite mercy, to the praise and glory of his own name. In other words, God desires to make his *mercy* the apex of his own glory in the eyes of all creation. It is the ultimate reason for the creation of the world and the plan of redemption. It is the ultimate reason we should believe he is ready to do a great work of grace in us!

Dana Olson, a pastor friend of mine, opened my eyes to this. He wrote:

> Prior to creation God had no means of revealing one pinnacle attribute of his glory, mercy. While he could within the fellowship of the Trinity express love and maintain justice, mercy inherently requires some injustice or inadequacy before loving-kindness can be expressed in forgiveness. For this reason God set in motion redemptive history—to manifest his glory by revealing this very capacity to redeem, mercy.[4]

God wants to do a work "to the praise of his glorious *grace*" (Ephesians 1:6). God wants to show us his grace so that we "might glorify God for his *mercy*" (Romans 15:9). This is precisely the reasoning of Romans 9:22-23: "What if God, desiring to show his wrath and to make known his power, has endured with much patience vessels of wrath prepared for destruction, in order to *make known the riches of his glory for vessels of mercy,* which he has prepared beforehand for glory . . . ?" In his final judgment God will display the power of his wrath. But God could not demonstrate his capacity for mercy apart from ordaining a world of sin and a way for redemption. He endures with great patience the impenitent, so that he can magnify his all-glorious mercy in the eyes of those who put their hope in him!

JOHN NEWTON'S GRAVESTONE

John Newton, author of the hymn "Amazing Grace," died in 1807, having accomplished much in his lifetime. But he saw it as God's Great Work in him. He made this his lasting testimony by having the following words put on his gravestone:

> John Newton, Clerk
> Once an Infidel and Libertine,
> A Servant of Slaves in Africa,
> Was, by the rich mercy of our Lord and Saviour
> JESUS CHRIST,
> Preserved, restored, pardoned,
> And appointed to preach the Faith
> He had long laboured to destroy[5]

Newton's "rich mercy" is the Great Work of the gospel. It was his life experience to seek it, discover it, live it, and proclaim it an amazing work of grace. The apostle Paul summarized the gospel in similar fashion:

And you, who once were alienated and hostile in mind, doing evil deeds, he has now reconciled in his body of flesh by his death, in order to present you holy and blameless and above reproach before him, if indeed you continue in the faith, stable and steadfast, not shifting from the hope of the gospel that you heard, which has been proclaimed in all creation under heaven, and of which I, Paul, became a minister (Colossians 1:21-23).

This summary we will consider again and again, in searching out the Great Work. It will be our anchor text. With this, along with God's winsome invitation and his bold promise, let us consider how God might desire to be glorified in our own human experience of his rich mercy.

THE HUMAN EXPERIENCE OF GOD'S OUTWORKING GRACE

In the outworking of God's grace, there comes a point when we begin to consider the matter of forgiveness and reconciliation as a matter of first importance. As we do, God encourages us to look to him and to search out the glory of his mercy.

GROUP STUDY QUESTIONS

1. Billy, Alice, Antoinette, and Eva each have their own reasons for needing to learn about God's forgiveness and ongoing grace. What stories do you have of people struggling with similar issues? What is your story; what draws you to consider the gospel at this time?

2. This chapter has raised lots of questions that will be addressed throughout the book. What questions do you bring to this study of the Great Work?

3. The apostle Paul says it is possible to believe the gospel in *vain* (1 Corinthians 15:2). According to this text, what constitutes a vain or worthless kind of faith? Describe a situation or pattern of behavior where someone's claims are dubious at best.

4. Isaiah 1:18 and Jeremiah 31:33-34 are two promises of God. What would faith in these promises cause us to do?

5. I have said that God has a chief motive within himself that is good news for seekers of God's grace. What is it, and why is it good news?

6. We are calling Colossians 1:21-23 the "anchor text" of this book. Outline the key truths of the Great Work according to this text. Compare your outline with the Table of Contents page of this book.

2

THE GREAT WORK DESIRED

Owning Up to Our Guilt

God touches the spring of penitence in men through many deep experiences, but the experience is always that of beholding a goodness that shames us.

—H. R. MACKINTOSH,
THE CHRISTIAN EXPERIENCE OF FORGIVENESS

Once you were alienated from God and were enemies in your minds because of your evil behavior.

—COLOSSIANS 1:21, NIV

The first-century biographer Plutarch said, "Medicine, to produce health, has to examine disease; and music, to create harmony, must investigate discord."[1] So the prerequisite work of God in grace is an examination of guilt. God, the surgeon of our souls, cuts deep into our natural pride to convict us of the reality of our guilt. The desirability of God's forgiveness can grow only as the deniability of our own sinfulness shrinks. In human experience, God's convicting work is evident in the humble confession that it prompts.

THE MOUSE'S SEARCH FOR THE CAT

Ask a hundred people if they want forgiveness, and a hundred people will say, "Yeah, sure. And can I have fries with that, and a large Pepsi?" They have no great sense of needing God's forgiveness but believe it would not hurt to have it in their pocket just in case. Religion is, I fear, most often practiced to buy off God's anger, to pay for a sin done, so that one is free to go on in it. We throw ourselves into church or confession as a burglar might throw a steak to a watchdog—to keep him at a safe distance. C. S. Lewis had his own witty way of describing the problem: "Amiable agnostics will talk cheerfully about 'man's search for God.' To me, as I then was, they might as well have talked about the mouse's search for the cat."[2]

Our natural belief about ourselves is that we are pretty darned good people, though we are not too proud to admit we have made a few mistakes along the way. This allows us to confess a little guilt, but in a self-flattering way. We say, "Well, I admit I'm not *perfect.*" We do not mean to be humble here, as in "Now, honey, remember, I'm not a perfect husband." We say it defensively: "Okay! I'm not perfect." Translation: "Other than a blemish or two, I sparkle. So get off my case!"

We also like to say, "I'm only human." By this we mean, "My sin should be excused because, as a human being, I really can't help it."

Even when we *feel* guilty, we do not believe it is because we *are* guilty. We consider other reasons. Perhaps it originates from an overly harsh parental upbringing. Maybe it stems from the old nuns in their stealth-winged hats; they *make* people feel guilty. The philosopher Friedrich Nietzsche (1844–1900) scorned the notion of guilt and blamed it on Christianity. Its emphasis on a human weakness, met with a weak Savior hammered to a rugged cross, he considered poison, something that was harmful to humans.[3] Less religion leads to less guilt.

A modern trend suggests that our feeling of guilt is due to our "inner child" not being affirmed enough when our entire body was less than four feet tall. Maybe this guilt originates from a chemical imbalance in the brain. Maybe it is just a delusion: we are hearing voices that are not real. Maybe it springs from low self-esteem, and we need to reprogram ourselves—stand in front of the mirror like the comic character, Stuart Smalley, and practice saying, "I'm good enough, I'm smart enough, and, doggone it, people like me!" We laugh, but maybe guilt comes from a sick perfectionism. A bubbling brew of all these explanations might explain the origin of our sense of guilt.

The solution, many suggest, is to treat guilt as a psychological condition. We look to therapists to sift through our memories until they find the clinker that set off our guilt, so we can remove it. We achieve success when we hear, "Really, there is no *justifiable* reason for you to feel guilty—it's not *your* fault." Plenty of books will tell us this, as will religious swamis. People spend thousands of dollars to confirm that the origin of their guilt is found in what somebody else did to hurt them.

Even when we own up to our actual guilt, we usually attempt to shift attention to our woundedness and away from our waywardness. We pray, "Forgive me, because I only sinned a little, and I only did it once, and only because so-and-so did such-and-such to me." This is a clever way of admitting to guilt while justifying it at the same time. Another way we put the best spin on guilt is to say, "God, forgive me. I really didn't mean it." In other words, we meant well. Our hearts were *good*. This prayer for forgiveness is based on our really *not* needing it. It's really a cry to be understood, not forgiven.

A STUNNING PRAYER!

It is stunning, then, to read how King David prayed: "For your name's sake, O LORD, pardon my guilt, for it is great" (Psalm 25:11). What a radical prayer! David prays in the exact opposite direction of most people. What is prayed for? God's *forgiveness*, not his understanding. What needs to be forgiven? Not my mistakes or my weaknesses but my *guilt*. Whose guilt needs God's forgiveness? *My very own.* Why should God forgive me? Because it's just a little sin? No! Because my guilt is *great!* And why should God forgive great sinners such as I? So that *the greatness of God's mercy* might become famous—"for your name's sake, O LORD." David pins his hope on owning up to the reality of his guilt and believing that God wants to magnify his mercy by forgiving David, to the praise of his name.

THE BIBLE CALLS US TO OWN UP TO OUR REAL GUILT

A good place to begin understanding the true reality of guilt and its consequences is Colossians 1:21: "And you, who once were alienated and hostile in mind, *doing evil deeds* . . . " Paul is about to point out how God forgives, but he starts with the problem. The guilt feelings and self-condemnation that play like a never ending cassette tape in our own minds originate from what we did—from "doing evil deeds." Not what our parents did. Not what society did. Not what God did in creating us. We feel guilty because we *know* that what we did was evil, even damnable.

Colossians 1:21 says more. It teaches us that our evil behavior has alienated us from a righteous God. We are "alienated and hostile in mind." It is not that we do not believe that God is good and loving. We do. It is that we feel *alienated* from God's goodness and love because of what we have done. It is not that we do not want his blessing. We would gladly receive it. It is that down deep, we fear that God is justified in withholding it. On this we should trust our feelings. For the painful truth is, we *feel* alienated from God because we *are* alienated from God. So Isaiah explains,

> Behold, the LORD's hand is not shortened, that it cannot save,
>   or his ear dull, that it cannot hear;
> but your iniquities have made a *separation*
>   between you and your God,
> and your sins have *hidden* his face from you
>   so that he does not hear.
> For your hands are defiled with blood
>   and your fingers with iniquity;
> your lips have spoken lies;
>   your tongue mutters wickedness. . . .

For our transgressions are multiplied before you,
    and our sins testify against us;
for our transgressions are with us,
    and we know our iniquities: . . .
Justice is *turned back,*
    and righteousness *stands afar off*;
for truth has stumbled in the public squares,
    and uprightness cannot enter (Isaiah 59:1-3, 12, 14).

Our sin separates us from God. It has left us alienated from him. His righteousness and love are put off by our evil. It is there, but it "stands afar off." It is not ours for the having.

OUR CONSCIENCE CALLS US TO OWN UP TO OUR REAL GUILT

The reality of this alienation is not only confirmed in Scripture, our conscience bears witness to it as well. Colossians 1:21 speaks of being "hostile *in mind,* doing evil deeds." *In our minds* we sense God's righteous displeasure and his judgment against us. The experience of guilt, then, is the videotape replay of our own evil behavior in the pretrial hearings that are held long before that final day of judgment. The pretrial hearing room is the human conscience.

Ole Hallesby was one of Norway's leading Christian teachers. He played a leading role in the church's opposition to the Nazis. It cost him two years in a concentration camp. He wrote, "The conscience is the simplest and clearest expression of the exalted character and dignity of human life. Here we touch upon something which makes man a man and exalts him above the animals."[4] Animals live by instinct. They do what they do without guilt feelings or remorse. A dog may put his tail between his legs when he is caught digging in the trash can, but a dog is not burdened by a guilty conscience. He may fear a scolding or regret that he got caught before he could reach the chicken bones, but he does not lie in his bed thinking, *Why did I do that? I know I'm not supposed to. I'm so ashamed. I wonder if my father snooped in the trash.* It is humanity alone that is endowed with a conscience by our Creator.

The conscience is that faculty by which we know, together with God, whether we are living in conformity to his good and perfect will for our lives. It bears witness that God is holy and righteous, and that it is right to love such a God and be like him. It confirms that "all have sinned and fall short of the glory of God" (Romans 3:23). Our conscience whispers that God is great and greatly to be praised and that it is wrong to ignore such a great God and go our own way.

The ancient Greek dramatist Menander (342–292 B.C.) said, "Conscience is a god to all mortals." Romans 2:14-15 confirms that conscience is at least the *voice* of God:

> For when Gentiles, who do not have the law, by nature do what the law requires, they are a law to themselves, even though they do not have the law. They show that the work of the law is written on their hearts, while their conscience also bears witness, and their conflicting thoughts accuse or even excuse them.

Through the conscience we sense the moral will of God and know something about our own conformity or conflict with it. In our minds (our consciences) we know our guilt is real. And in our hearts (our consciences, again) we sense the hostility between us and God.

It is important to note that this knowledge is shared. We know it *together with God*. Through my conscience I sense not only right and wrong but God's pleasure or displeasure as well. When I lie, I know I have done wrong. I also know that God knows I lied. I also know that he agrees with my conscience that I have done wrong. And I know that God knows that I know I have done wrong.

Thus there begins a straining of relationship between God and me. My sinful behavior is registered in my conscience as guilt before God and causes us both to withdraw from each other. I withdraw because I sense the reality of my sinfulness and, in light of his righteousness, I fear God's judgment. God withdraws out of faithfulness to his own righteousness. As Isaiah said, "Righteousness stands afar off" (Isaiah 59:14).

YOU'RE HURTING MY SELF-ESTEEM

One reason it is hard for us to own up to the reality of human guilt is that it runs contrary to the therapeutic models of sin. The dominant social theory of the day says that self-worth, self-respect, and self-esteem are the cure for antisocial behavior. William Kilpatrick, a professor of educational psychology, writes, "This business of liking oneself has become for us almost a first principle. It seems self-evident, in the same category with 'the sky is blue.' No one is inclined to dispute it. Psychology, of course, didn't invent the notion, but it has capitalized on it. You might say it is the 'good news' of the psychological gospel."[5]

According to modern theories of self-esteem, guilt feelings poison a person's ability to feel good about himself or herself. Feeling good about ourselves is vital to good behavior. If a teenager is rude, violent, and out of control it is because he has low self-esteem. He should not be punished, and he must never be made to feel ashamed. He needs a higher view of himself. People with high self-esteem have no reason to lash out and hurt others. This is axiomatic among social workers, educators, and youth workers.

There is a sense of worthlessness that affects some people that is entirely unhealthy and unbiblical. I think especially of the self-loathing associated with anorexia. Such a person is focused on self-punishment. All people have an intrinsic value as people made in the image of God. Jesus pointed this out when he said, "Of how much more value are you than the birds!" (Luke 12:24). The problem with self-loathing, however, is that it is still an expression of self-*centeredness*. The cure will not come by exchanging one kind of self-centeredness for another. To the degree that self-love denies the inherent and willful capacity to do wrong, it denies the reality of our guilt and undercuts seeking God's grace.

What do we make, then, of human beings being compared to worms? God called Israel a worm (Isaiah 41:14). The context here is the contrast between Israel's helplessness and God's helpfulness. Israel is threatened by her enemies to be crushed (like a worm.) But God assures Israel, "Fear not, you worm Jacob, you men of Israel! I am the one who helps you, declares the LORD" (41:14). There is nothing unseemly or unhealthy here. It is comfort for the weak, by a strong defender.

In a similar context, Paul wrote, "*Wretched* man that I am!" (Romans 7:24). In context, Paul is considering his delight in the supremacy of God and bemoaning the law of sin in himself that steadfastly undercuts his loving so great a God wholeheartedly.

John Newton wrote the famous hymn "Amazing Grace":

Amazing grace! How sweet the sound, that saved a wretch like me!
I once was lost but now I'm found, was blind but now I see.

Newton was not suffering from low self-esteem when he called himself a wretch. Rather, he was drunk with the grandeur of God's mercy to forgive sinners.

Isaac Watts wrote another of the church's favorite hymns, "Alas. And Did My Savior Bleed?"

Alas! And did my Savior bleed? And did my Sovereign die?
Would he devote that sacred head for such a worm as I?[6]

In calling himself a worm, Watts is saying that he knows himself to be a guilty sinner, one given over to sin. He is acknowledging that there is no moral goodness *in himself* that motivated Christ's death on his behalf.

Someone may object, "God loves me. Christ died for me. Therefore I must be really valuable to God since he paid so high a price for me." Indeed, it is more common than not to hear the cross of Christ proclaimed in this self-esteem-inflating way. But Romans 5:8 says something very different: "But God shows his love for us in that while we were still sinners, Christ died for us." It is true that God's love compelled him to send his Son into the world to die for our sins (see also John 3:16). It is *not* true that his love for us, expressed in the cross, is motivated chiefly by our inherent value and goodness. Christ's death for us is chiefly motivated by the value he places on *himself* and his own glory as a loving God. His chief motivation is to display his loving-kindness or mercy, as the glorious thing it is before all creation, that we might taste and enjoy his value, not our own. To accomplish this, he displays a love so awesome and far-reaching that it can love the unlovely.

Paul would never say, "The fact that Jesus died for me shows me how valuable I am to God." Instead, he was amazed because he saw himself as the "worst of sinners":

> The saying is trustworthy and deserving of full acceptance, that Christ Jesus came into the world to save sinners, of whom *I am the foremost.* But I received *mercy* for this reason, that in me, as the foremost, Jesus Christ might *display his perfect patience* as an example to those who were to believe in him for eternal life (1 Timothy 1:15-16).

According to Paul, it was not something in himself that motivated Christ's sacrifice, it was something in God. What was it? "I received mercy for this reason, that in me . . . Jesus Christ might display *his perfect patience.*" Paul saw and *delighted* in the reality that God's forgiveness highlighted the excellency of God's patience, not his own goodness or worth. God loves us as guilty sinners, not as *Somebodies.*

THE PRINCESS WHO WAS A SOMEBODY

George MacDonald wrote "The Wise Woman or the Lost Princess," a wonderful children's story that illustrates that, when it comes to self, more is worse, and less is best:

> A baby girl was born; and her father was a king and her mother was a queen. . . . So the little girl was a Somebody. As she grew up, everybody about her did his best to convince her that she was Somebody; and the girl herself was so easily persuaded of it that she quite forgot that anybody had ever told her so, and took it for a fundamental, innate, primary, first-born, self-evident, necessary, and incontrovertible idea and principle that she was Somebody. And far be it from me to deny it. I will even go so far as to assert that in this odd country there was a huge number of Somebodies; and the worst

of it was that the princess never thought of there being more than one Somebody—and that was herself.[7]

The story goes on to describe how the princess's self-love leads to terrible behavior—she throws tantrums and mistreats others. All evil behavior is motivated by an overinflated sense of self-worth that supplants the worth of God and the worth of others. That is written into the genetic code of every sinful action: me first, me last, glory be to me. Frederick Buechner said it well: "We all tend to make ourselves the center of the universe."[8]

We live in a world where everybody looks to everybody else to make himself or herself happy. To paraphrase psychologist Larry Crabb, everybody is a tick in search of a dog![9] In searching for God's forgiveness, we must not pin our hopes on God finding us so valuable that he feels compelled to forgive us. We must pin our hopes on God wanting to show us the value of his love for guilty sinners.

IF I STEAL, AM I A THIEF?

When we break the moral law of God, we become *lawbreakers*. When I sin, I confirm that I am by nature a *sinner*. When I was a teenager, I stole a hat from a store. I did not lack self-esteem. I lacked a hat that I wanted. What is worse, I arrived at the store with a wad of money in my pocket from a newspaper job I had. Staring at the price tag, I thought, *Hey, why should I spend my money, money I worked so hard to get, on that hat? I can get it for nothing by pinching it, then save my money for something else.* Far from lacking self-esteem, I greatly esteemed my own keen insight at that moment!

As I headed for the door, the store manager stopped me. I turned six shades of green and wished I were dead. The manager saw I was not yet a hardened criminal and sent me home with instructions to have my parents call him back with the news or he would call the police. I went home to take my lumps. To this day, I remember what my eighteen-year-old sister said when she overheard me confessing. With disgust dripping from her voice, she said, "How totally embarrassing. I've got a brother who's a thief!"

She called me a thief! Clearly she did not know that this could make me worse, by damaging my self-image. Shouldn't she have tried to build up my self-esteem by saying, "You know, you're really a great kid, and I'm so glad you're my brother. You're a very special person, and stealing is beneath you"? She said in effect, "You're nothing but a stupid sinner, and you should be ashamed of yourself."

Becoming ashamed of what we are as a result of what we do is a good and necessary part of getting real about guilt. If you murder, you become a murderer. If you commit adultery, you are an adulterer. If you lie, you become a liar. If you steal, you are a thief, not "a person of low self-esteem." I stole, and I had become a thief. It led me to my room weeping and ashamed of myself. But that was good! Painful, but good.

MY NAME IS LEGION

The reality is, all of us have sinned and are guilty before God. You may have done some things I have not done, and vice versa, but in the end we are partners in crime in need of pardon. C. S. Lewis was an English scholar and a resolved atheist for many years prior to becoming a celebrated Christian apologist and writer. He wanted to be an atheist because he wanted to keep his independence. He called God the *Interferer*. But to justify his independence from God, he felt that "an attempt at complete virtue must be made" (then he would not need God or his forgiveness). Of this effort he wrote:

> Really, a young atheist cannot guard his faith too carefully. Dangers lie in wait for him on every side. You must not do, you must not even try to do, the will of the Father unless you are prepared to "know of the doctrine." All my acts, desires, and thoughts were to be brought into harmony with universal Spirit. For the first time I examined myself with a seriously practical purpose. And there I found what appalled me; a zoo of lusts, a bedlam of ambitions, a nursery of fears, a harem of fondled hatreds. My name was legion.[10]

When Lewis says we must be prepared to "know the doctrine," he means that if we would enjoy the beauty of holiness we must first own up to the reality of our sinful nature. "If we say we have not sinned, we make [God] a liar, and his word is not in us" (1 John 1:10). This means that, in denying the reality of our own sinfulness, we are also sinning. We are accusing God of lying when he calls us guilty sinners. This makes God evil. If, then, God is evil, truly we are beyond hope. If we accuse the God of all glory of being evil, surely we will regret the day he comes to vindicate the goodness of his name.

BEHOLDING A GOODNESS THAT SHAMES US

Ultimately, God shows us the reality of our guilt by showing us the purity of his goodness. H. R. Mackintosh said, "God touches the spring of penitence in men through many deep experiences, but the experience is always that of beholding a goodness that shames us."[11] God is good, and everything he does reflects his goodness. "Good and upright is the LORD" (Psalm 25:8). "You [God] are good and do good" (Psalm 119:68).

Isaiah saw the goodness of the Lord and shouted, "Woe is me!"

> *I saw the Lord* sitting upon a throne, high and lifted up; and the train of his robe filled the temple. Above him stood the seraphim. Each had six wings: with two he covered his face, and with two he covered his feet, and with two he flew. And one called to another and said:
>
> > "Holy, holy, holy is the LORD of hosts;
> > the whole earth is full of his glory!" (Isaiah 6:1-3).

The light of God's goodness revealed the cracks in Isaiah's character:

> *And I said: "Woe is me!* For I am lost; for I am a man of unclean lips, and I dwell in the midst of a people of unclean lips; for my eyes have seen the King, the LORD of hosts!" (6:5).

When we see the God of glory, the ugly reality of our sin becomes self-evident. Until brilliant white paint is put on the wall, the old off-white looks fairly white. But before God the truth of ourselves is laid bare.

At that moment we will run or we will kneel. In kneeling we are owning up to our guilt. Jesus once advised, "Come to terms quickly with your accuser" (Matthew 5:25). In this case our accuser is God himself. In kneeling we are agreeing with God.

Our conscience, also, accuses us of sinful behavior; it blames us for doing evil and becoming evil. We agree with our conscience. The Word of God indicts us for being self-seeking, rejecting the truth, and following evil (Romans 2:8). We agree with Scripture.

Because we now agree that we feel guilty because we *are* guilty, we will also *agree with God in prayer*. Daniel's prayer is an example of the kind of confession we need to bring to God:

> Then I turned my face to the Lord God, seeking him by prayer and pleas for mercy with fasting and sackcloth and ashes. I prayed to the LORD my God and made confession, saying, "O Lord, the great and awesome God, who keeps covenant and steadfast love with those who love him and keep his commandments, we have sinned and done wrong and acted wickedly and rebelled, turning aside from your commandments and rules. We have not listened to your servants. . . . To you, O Lord, belongs righteousness, but to us open shame . . . because we have sinned against you. To the Lord our God belong mercy and forgiveness, for we have rebelled against him and have not obeyed the voice of the LORD our God by walking in his laws, which he set before us by his servants the prophets. . . . O Lord, hear; O Lord, forgive" (Daniel 9:3-6a, 7a, 8b-10, 19).

We need to pray in the same radical direction King David prayed:

> For your name's sake, O LORD,
> Pardon my guilt, for it is great (Psalm 25:11).

In owning up to the reality of his guilt, C. S. Lewis saw this as something God was doing in him. He saw it as God's convicting work—a hard but necessary part of the Great Work of the gospel. "The hardness of God is kinder than the softness of men," he wrote, "and His compulsion is our liberation."[12]

The Human Experience of God's Outworking Grace

The early work of God's grace consists of God convicting us of the reality of our sin and the separation, hostility, and enmity that truly exists between us and him. Our human experience of God's outworking grace is our painful acknowledgment of the truth of our personal guilt and our humble confession of sin before God in prayer.

GROUP STUDY QUESTIONS

1. According to Colossians 1:21, why do people feel guilty? How does our guilt affect our relationship with God? How can we tell that things between us and God are not naturally good and friendly—what are some of the signs of our alienation from him?

2. Which do you spend more time focused on, your woundedness or your waywardness? Why is it so hard for us to admit our own guilt? What are some of the common ways you deal with a guilty conscience? What guilt can you admit to now?

3. What is so radical about David's prayer in Psalm 25:11?

4. I have recalled George MacDonald's story of the girl who thought she was a "Somebody." What truth does this story illustrate that is vital to a biblical understanding of the Great Work? What am I arguing against in telling this story, when it comes to self-esteem? Do you agree with my conclusion that the gospel is God-centered, not man-centered?

5. I have told how stealing a hat led me to admit that I was a "sinner." How have you yourself come to this painful discovery? What in Daniel's prayer (Daniel 9:3-10, 19) seems appropriate in your own case?

3

THE GREAT WORK NEEDED

Acknowledging the Justice of God's Judgment

> O Conscience, into what abyss of fears
> And horrors hast thou driven me; out of which
> I find no way, from deep to deeper plunged.
> —JOHN MILTON, *PARADISE LOST*

> God is a righteous judge,
>   a God who expresses his wrath every day.
> —PSALM 7:11, NIV

Some years ago I had the joy of going to Saint Croix in the Virgin Islands with a team of twenty men and women from my church. We went to rebuild roofs for the impoverished people on the island after a devastating hurricane. We worked like oil riggers but had great joy in our service. On our off day, I went snorkeling in the bluest water I had ever seen. Right below me in twenty feet of pristine water teemed schools of neon blue and yellow fish darting in and out of bone-white castles of living coral and purple-fanned plants.

Flooded with a sense of the beauty and the glory of God as our magnificent Creator, I started slapping the surface of the water and yelling praises through my snorkel. My muffled hollering attracted the attention of the three men with me. At first they thought I was drowning. Soon they caught on to my delight and joined me in slapping the water and whooping it up to the praise of God above for the beauty he displayed below us. Then I swam out a little farther.

Another hundred yards out, the coral ended abruptly as the water's depth increased. No radiant colored fish were in sight. The rock turned barren and flat. Suddenly, and I do mean suddenly, the rock curved straight down into a gripping black abyss. Tiny candles of light shafts danced below me to a depth that I could not measure. Below that, only a dread darkness with no visible bottom.

A dread fear squeezed the air right out of my lungs. I trembled at the abyss and bolted, like a duckling seeing his first alligator, for the safety of the shoreline. As I swam away from the abyss and over the beauty of the coral garden, I could not help but recall the gripping words of Romans 11:22: "Note then the kindness and the *severity* of God." (Later I learned that I was looking at and swimming right above the island's continental shelf, which descends toward the famous Puerto Rico Trench. The ocean floor drops to a depth of 12,600 feet at this point—almost two and a half miles deep! Sharks feed along the edge. What swims at the bottom swims without eyes, for there is no light.)

What can we say about the severity of God? What is the wrath of God? How do we square the love of God in Christ ("For God so *loved* the world, that he gave his only Son"—John 3:16) with the harsh warnings of Scripture and the dread descriptions of final judgment? What is it, in terms of the outworking of God's forgiveness, that God intends for us in the revelation of his fierce and terrible wrath?

A SHOCKING DISCOVERY

The wrath of God revealed in the Bible is so terrible, so fierce, so awful, that it forces us to reach a shocking conclusion: either our sin and guilt is far, far greater than we ever knew, or God's punishment far, far exceeds the crime. If we conclude the latter then our mostly hidden resentment of God's sovereign authority over us will break out into the open. "I could never love a God like that! I will never trust or obey a God who wields such terrible threats over us to induce us to serve him." If we conclude that God is just and believe that his punishments always fit the crime, then we will have made the frightful discovery of what the old preachers called "the *exceeding* sinfulness of sin."

THE JUSTICE OF GOD'S JUDGMENT

Romans 1:18-23 declares the justice of God's judgment by declaring the depth of our guilt. It explains *what* we have done wrong, *why* it is intensely wrong, and *why* God is right to be angry with us:

> For the wrath of God is revealed from heaven against all ungodliness and unrighteousness of men, who by their unrighteousness suppress the truth. For what can be known about God is plain to them, because God has shown it to them. For his invisible attributes, namely, his eternal power and divine nature, have been clearly perceived, ever since the creation of the world, in the things that have been made. So they are without excuse. For although they knew God, they did not honor him as God or give thanks to him, but they became futile in their thinking, and their foolish hearts were darkened. Claiming to be wise, they became fools, and exchanged the glory of the immortal God for images resembling mortal man and birds and animals and reptiles.

There is much to trace out here. If we have thought only superficially about our sin, we have probably thought only superficially about God. This text does require some hard thinking. I find it helpful to break it out according to the questions it answers.

1. What is God's response to our sinful behavior? God's wrath. It is his response to "all ungodliness and unrighteousness" (1:18).

2. What sin have we committed that deserves the wrath of God? We have suppressed the truth. All forms of human sinfulness are merely different and compounding ways that we suppress the truth. "For the wrath of God is revealed from heaven against all ungodliness and unrighteousness of men, *who by their unrighteousness suppress the truth*" (1:18).

3. *What truth is suppressed by our evil behavior?* The truth of what "can be known about God" (1:19). In other words, every act of sin is a way of suppressing or rejecting the enormous truth of God himself.

4. *What can be known about God?* That he is an infinitely glorious, omnipotent, holy, and benevolent God. These and other "invisible attributes" (1:20) are rejected in every act of unrighteousness. Sin is rejecting the glory of God.

5. *What proof is there that we are suppressing the truth of God's infinite beauty, sovereign power, perfect holiness, and generous nature?* First, we have refused to *glorify him as God and thank him for his goodness.* "For although they knew God, *they did not honor him as God or give thanks to him*" (1:21). And second, we have exchanged the glory of God for lesser things. Human sin is exceedingly sinful in that it suppresses the truth of the glory of God and instead turns to lesser things to love and praise.

6. *Why is this an infinitely heinous evil?* Because God has revealed the truth of his infinite glory *plainly* and *clearly* through what he has made. "For his invisible attributes, namely, his eternal power and divine nature, have been clearly perceived, ever since the creation of the world, *in the things that have been made*" (1:20).

The conclusion then is brought home. There is "no excuse" for not glorifying God and not being thankful for his goodness toward us (1:20). The infinite greatness of God's glory—his excellence, splendor, beauty, power, wisdom, and benevolence—is so self-evident that not seeing it requires effort, a defiant refusal to see it. Robert Murray McCheyne, a vibrant preacher in England, who died at the age of twenty-nine in 1843, wrote, "Sin is an infinite evil because it is the breaking of an infinite obligation. Surely there are none that would say that God is not infinitely lovely; and therefore none will say that there is not an infinite obligation upon us to serve him. Then if you and I do not do this, we are breaking an infinite obligation; and if it be an infinite evil then it demands infinite punishment."[1] We can test the truthfulness of this by checking out how visible God's glory is. The more evident the truth is, as the Westminster Confession puts it, "that the whole duty of man is to glorify God and enjoy him forever," then the more evil it is not to have done so.

SURROUNDED BY GOD'S GLORY

God has revealed his glory in at least three plentiful and pleasing ways. First, he has revealed it *plainly* and *clearly* in all that he has made. Creation's grandeur speaks of the grandeur of the Creator. The art reflects the artist. The twinkling galaxies speak of God's inexhaustible nature. The wheat field declares his benevolence. As the Yiddish proverb says, "He who gives us teeth, will give us bread."[2] Every created thing has its own language, but the translation is the same: "Great is the Lord and worthy to be praised!"

> The heavens *declare* the glory of God,
> and the sky above proclaims his handiwork.
> Day to day pours out speech,
> and night to night reveals knowledge.
> There is no speech, nor are there words,
> whose voice is not heard.
> Their measuring line goes out through all the earth,
> and their words to the end of the world (Psalm 19:1-4).

A second way that God reveals his glory plainly and visibly is in the creation of mankind. "God created man in his own image" (Genesis 1:27). The glory of God is uniquely imprinted into every human life to reflect his glory and refract it for all to see. So far God has created billions of image-bearers—more than six billion inhabit the earth at present—all designed to disseminate his glory in the world.

How do we echo God's glory as human beings? When men and women look to God and say, "Wow!" whether in praise or in silent meditation, we echo God's *delight* in his own goodness. When we refrain from evil, we reflect God's *moral* glory. When we help the poor and defend the innocent, we image God's *benevolent* glory. When we imprison lawbreakers, we reflect God's *judicial* glory. As stewards over the earth, we reflect his *reigning* glory. When we proclaim pardon for the guilty through Jesus Christ, we refract his *redemptive* glory.

The third way God surrounds us with evidence of his great power and the invisible qualities of his nature is through the benevolence he originally bestowed on mankind. From the moment Adam took his first breath, God demonstrated that his glory was a *benevolent glory*. Everything God made for Adam was set in place with the refrain, "And God saw that it was *good*" (Genesis 1:4, 10, 12, 18). And when he finished, "God saw everything that he had made, and behold, it was *very good*" (1:31).

Adam lived amid a rich variety of God-created trees and animals. He was provided food and meaningful labor. When that was not enough, God created Eve from Adam, so that he might *enjoy* a level of intimacy and partnership unique to them above all the rest of creation. Together they were to live under God's benevolent rule, trusting in his goodness and *enjoying* his provision (Genesis 2). Everything around them echoed, "God will provide!" (see Genesis 22:8).

The faith we are to place in God is a glad willingness to trust that he will provide for us everything that will truly make us happy in the long run. "Do not be deceived. . . . Every good gift and every perfect gift is from above, coming down from the Father of lights with whom there is no variation or shadow due to change" (James 1:16-17). The vegetable soup, hot rolls, and butter we eat on cold winter nights can be traced to his goodness toward us. He provides work, often (though not always) productive and fulfilling, to pay our bills. Out of his goodness come brotherly friendship, marriage, and family.

The truth that God is a *glorious* God and *worthy* to be praised is panoramically laid out in creation. It is stamped on the unique face of every coworker, neighbor, and family member we see. And it is reaffirmed every day by God's benevolent provision for us. To live according to this truth would mean that we rejoice in the goodness of God and live to the praise of his glory.

DESPISING GOD'S GLORY

No one has the excuse of saying, "I did not know that God wanted a relationship with me marked by my thankfulness for his goodness to me." We did know it; we just suppressed it. Then we went further: we replaced God altogether with a god of our own imagination. Romans 1:23 says, "[We] exchanged the glory of the immortal God for images resembling mortal man and birds and animals and reptiles." Herein lies the offensiveness of sin, the wrath-provoking nature of it.

It is like a man landing a job at the White House. He is appointed to serve the president in promoting the public good and sees it as the very great honor it is. He is excited to think that his service is going to advance the reputation of the president and his administration. He is a part of history. But instead of being thankful to the president and serving him gladly, suppose the man refuses to acknowledge the president or form public policy "in his name." Suppose instead he foolishly starts serving the White House cat and pretending she is the one in charge! He creates a wide variety of policies he thinks the cat-president wants.

For this man, everything is peachy except those brief moments when his pretense breaks down and he thinks of the day when the real president decides he has put up with the stupidity and insults and treasonous behavior long enough. He knows the day will come. Nothing, not even the good things the man did in the name of the cat, will matter on that dreadful day. So he flushes the thought of it from his head and fetches cream and kibbles for the cat.

No matter how bizarre this sounds, it is akin to the nature of our rebellion against God. He is the God of infinite glory. He has made his glory known in awesome and satisfying ways. We were made to know him and serve him. But we have rejected this service as worthless and "exchanged the glory of the immortal God for images resembling mortal man and birds and animals and reptiles" (Romans 1:23). No wonder we are terrified at the prospect of meeting God one day.

Though out of fashion in most of the secularized West, much of the world still is marked by idols made from stone and wood, fashioned into various animal images. God declares, "I am the LORD your God. . . . have no other gods before [meaning *besides*] me" (Exodus 20:2-3). This includes making gods of ourselves. Claiming to be wise and beyond the myths of religion, we love to "exchange the glory of the immortal God for images resembling mortal man," especially when the image is the person in the mirror! We worship our own will as our highest authority. Only later do we discover that by abandoning God, we become godless, and soon after, we ourselves become wicked gods.

A WICKED GOD

Vera was an eighteen-year-old unwed mother. She grew up in a church in Boston's inner city where her grandfather served as pastor. Once I delivered a sermon titled "How to Grow Up in the Church and Still Find God," because I know that even kids like Vera get confused and dragged away. Vera got involved with a young man who shared none of her faith and values. It did not take long before Vera's values gave way.

Her pregnancy was a turning point. She put her hope in God. Months later, Vera came by our local pregnancy help center with her three-month-old, beautiful baby son. The center provided her baby supplies and encouraged her to hold fast to God and her moral values. The notes of her visit recorded that she had adopted an abstinent lifestyle because of her recommitment to Christ and was attempting to break off the abusive relationship she had with the baby's father. She wanted a peaceful home.

She is at peace now, but not in the way we expected. A few days after her last visit, Vera was stabbed repeatedly with a knife and bled to death outside her apartment three blocks away from my home. After murdering Vera, her boyfriend attempted to rape another woman and was arrested. At Vera's funeral we wept and grieved with her family.

How could this happen? The biblical answer is that a man suppressed the truth about God, became godless, and became a wicked god.

His crime, however, is even greater than murder. He murdered Vera *and* defaced the glory of God that she imaged. "You shall not murder," declares the Decalogue. By this commandment God establishes the value he places on human life. The act of murder says, "God, what you call valuable, I call worthless. Your glory is worthless, and so is your command." But what does God say? "I made Vera an image-bearer of my own glory! I will not let you demean or deface my glory!

I will utterly crush and defeat you and vindicate both Vera and my glory!" In other words, "For the *wrath* of God is revealed from heaven against all ungodliness and unrighteousness of men" (Romans 1:18).

GOD'S WRATH IS A SENSIBLE AND JUSTIFIED ANGER

God's wrath flows from holiness. He is unable to tolerate or to "look at" wrong (Habakkuk 1:13). While human comparisons are faulty, there is such a thing as righteous indignation in human relationships. For example, when someone defaces a Jewish gravestone with a painted swastika, society is right to be angry. We are not angry over the need to buy paint remover. We are angry because it defaces human life, and in this case in a way that reasserts the evil of the Holocaust. Our wrath is necessary and healthy. Love must be able to get angry as well as to comfort.

If I come across a man raping a woman, I cannot love both of them in the same way—and neither can God. Love is inherently *moral* in character. I cannot go up to the struggling, terrorized woman and the overpowering assailant and say, "I love you both just the same, and so does God. He does not want you to harm this girl, but please do not think he is angry at you right now. Because God is love, he does not get mad. Isn't such a love amazing?" The woman would denounce my love as sick and worthless, even cowardly and evil. She would know that love must have a *passionate commitment* to right over wrong. It must be willing to vindicate and disarm; to reward and punish. To act in love in this situation I must *hate* what the attacker is doing and push him aside, scream my lungs out for help, grab the woman, and run.

The punishment later dispensed in a court of law validates the respect and love we hold for the woman. It affirms her honor. It helps her heal from her wounds.

Even in the course of our normal social life, we sense the rightness of holy anger. Consider how demeaned we can feel and offended we can become when someone merely slights us or ignores us. How quick we are to react, even though we are not holy or all-glorious like

God. Imagine, then, what an enormous offense it is to deface the glory of God by our evil behavior! The sin is as great as God's glory is great. This and nothing less than this is the degree of offense committed in *every* act of sin.[3] King David saw this. All his sins boiled down to one wretched and damnable sin: defying God's rule over his life. In response he prayed,

> Against you, you only, have I sinned
> and done what is evil in your sight,
> so that you may be justified in your words
> and blameless in your judgment (Psalm 51:4).

BACK TO THE DAY I STOLE THE HAT

In the previous chapter, I told of the day I stole a hat. Let us go back a moment and apply what God says in Romans 1 to my petty theft. God's response to me might go like this: "John, you have sinned against your fellow man, who is trying to provide for his family. You have hurt him, and this is wrong. It is all the more wrong because I have called you to love your neighbor, and you know this. By stealing you have said to me, 'Your commands mean nothing to me.' Your stealing also says that you do not believe that I can be trusted to provide for you everything that will bring you true and lasting happiness. This is a great insult, and it makes me angry. Therefore, do not think that my wrath is coming on you for stealing a three-dollar hat. It is coming on you for defying my rightful authority over you. It is coming on you for demeaning my *trustworthiness*."

A just punishment for stealing a hat might be to return it and pay a fine of thirty dollars. But what is the just penalty for defacing the eternal glory of God except an eternal punishment?

Our difficulty in seeing the enormity of this sin reflects how far our thoughts have sunk from the glory of God. We thought our problem was that God might not be impressed with us as much as we would like him to be. We have a few bad marks on an otherwise good record. We have worried that even those few bad marks might cause us a problem with God—after all, he does have high standards. So we try to do a little "extra credit" work to impress him. But in truth, the problem is that we have not been impressed with *him*. We want God to marvel at us when, in reality, we ought to marvel at him! That is the sin that damns us.

The implication is astounding, and Romans 14:23 confirms it: "For whatever does not proceed from faith is sin." To me, this is the most shocking truth in the Bible, because it completely demolishes any hope that God might be impressed with some of what I do and that he might use that to form the basis of forgiving and accepting me. Instead, I find that *all* of what I do is forming the basis of my condemnation because all of what I do is done in an effort to supplant the glory of God with my own—and this is a form of robbery. Every second I put off living for the glory of God, I am only adding to the justice of God's fierce wrath against me.

The enormity of our sin consists of this exchange of affection from seeking the glory of God to a self-seeking glory. God declares boldly that for those who are "self-seeking and do not obey the truth, but obey unrighteousness, there will be wrath and fury" (Romans 2:8).

THE WRATH OF GOD, WITHOUT APOLOGIES

God declares the fierceness of his wrath without apologies. Isaiah declared the *certainty and intensity* of it:

> Behold, the day of the LORD comes,
>   cruel, *with wrath and fierce anger,*
> to make the land a desolation
>   and to destroy its sinners from it.
> For the stars of the heavens and their constellations
>   will not give their light;
> the sun will be dark at its rising,
>   and the moon will not shed its light.
> I will punish the world for its evil,
>   and the wicked for their iniquity; . . .
> I will make people more rare than fine gold,
>   and mankind than the gold of Ophir.
> Therefore I will make the heavens tremble,
>   and the earth will be shaken out of its place,

at the wrath of the LORD of hosts
   in the day of his fierce anger (Isaiah 13:9-13).

Zephaniah described the *bitterness* of God's wrath.

"The great day of the LORD is near,
   near and hastening fast;
the sound of the day of the LORD is bitter;
   the mighty man cries aloud there.
A day of wrath is that day,
   a day of distress and anguish,
a day of ruin and devastation . . .
   because they have sinned against the LORD" (1:14-15, 17).

Lest we delude ourselves that wrath is just a feature of "the Old Testament God," it is sobering to read in the New Testament,

For you may be sure of this, that everyone who is sexually immoral or impure, or who is covetous (that is, an idolater), has no inheritance in the kingdom of Christ and God. Let no one deceive you with empty words, for because of these things the wrath of God comes upon the sons of disobedience (Ephesians 5:5-6).

God's wrath is described as "fierce" (1 Samuel 28:18), "overflowing" (Job 40:11), "stirred up" (Psalm 78:38), "consuming" (Psalm 59:13), and "jealous" (Ezekiel 36:6). Various images are used to describe God's wrath. In Revelation 14:19-20 it is "the great winepress." In Jude 13 (NIV) it is "blackest darkness." In Isaiah 10:5 we read, "the staff in their hands is my fury!" The most commonly used metaphor for God's wrath is fire (e.g., Psalm 21:9; Lamentations 2:4). Consider then the *burning* anger of the Lord:

Who can stand before his indignation?
   Who can endure the heat of his anger?
His wrath is poured out like fire,
   and the rocks are broken into pieces by him (Nahum 1:6).

There comes a day when God deals with our sins. When it comes, it feels like fire.

THE WRATH OF GOD ACCORDING TO JESUS CHRIST

The most terrifying words of divine wrath revealed in the Bible, however, come from the mouth of Jesus—and properly so. As W. G. T. Shedd wrote,

> As none but God has the right and would dare to sentence a soul to eternal misery for sin . . . so none but God has the right and should presume to delineate the nature and consequences of this sentence. This is the reason why most of the awful imagery in which the sufferings of the wicked are described is found in the discourses of our Lord and Savior.[4]

It is Jesus who says to the uncaring and self-seeking, "Depart from me, you cursed, into the eternal fire prepared for the devil and his angels. For I was hungry and you gave me no food, I was thirsty and you gave me no drink" (Matthew 25:41-42). It is Jesus who warns us to take repentance seriously by saying, "If your eye causes you to sin, tear it out. It is better for you to enter the kingdom of God with one eye than with two eyes to be thrown into hell" (Mark 9:47).

To Jesus, hell is God's wrath with no admixture of mercy—"where their worm does not die and the fire is not quenched" (Mark 9:48). Hell is, according to Jesus, the worst condemnation imaginable. Its purpose is not remedial but punitive. The punishment is not temporary but eternal. Jesus said, "And these will go away into *eternal punishment,* but the righteous into eternal life" (Matthew 25:46).[5] Hell represents God's final response to persistent unbelief, when human depravity has reached full maturity and every loving warning sent has been rejected (Luke 16:19-31). Hell signals that there is a time when God's patience with *unrepentant* sinners runs out. There comes a time when God conquers the wicked because they will not turn and seek his forgiveness.

While hell itself is not corrective, the warnings of hell are so intended. Jesus speaks of God's wrath and talks graphically of hell to convince us to take our sin seriously and to induce us to turn from our sin and seek the forgiveness of God. This is grace at work! Where this grace is spurned, there is nothing but God's *final* judgment.

MISCONCEPTIONS ABOUT THE JUDGMENT OF GOD

There are many false perceptions about the wrath of God and the nature of hell. God's wrath is unlike human wrath. God is slow to anger. Hell is described as a place of fire; but so is heaven (Revelation 1:14). That is because God is a consuming fire (Hebrews 12:29). Each of us will one day encounter either his *blazing* love or his *burning* wrath.

Several years ago I attended an evangelistic crusade. The preacher wanted to affirm the loving-kindness of Christ and at the same time affirm the reality of hell. The two appeared incompatible to him. So he explained, "God does not send people to hell. They choose to go there." This statement has a certain attractiveness to it. It affirms the reality of hell but appears to take God off the hook in terms of being personally accountable for the actual damnation involved. But is this a biblically accurate explanation of the tension? I think not. The statement is distorted in several ways.

First, it uses the term *people* in reference to God's final judgment. The Bible does not generally use the term *people* with reference to God's judgment. The term *people* is used to describe what we have in common with each other as created beings, without any reference to our moral character. We talk of the people in our neighborhood. Our coworkers are people. People make up a crowd gathered in a football stadium, or an entire city or nation—the Chinese people, for example. No moral distinctions are made. Nothing is known or stated about any individual's moral goodness.[6] It is people we see dying of starvation. We are moved because we see them as fellow human beings made in the image of God.

When speaking of God's final judgment, the Bible uses a variety of terms that reflects the substance and foundation of our moral nature. We are called the "righteous" or the "wicked." God's judgment is not on people but on the *wicked*. So we read, "The *wicked* will be cut off from the land" (Proverbs 2:22) and "The LORD's curse is on the house of the *wicked*, but he blesses the dwelling of the *righteous*" (Proverbs 3:33). In the same way, Jesus said, "So it will be at the close of the age. The angels will come out and separate the *evil* from the *righteous* and throw them into the fiery furnace. In that place there will be weeping and gnashing of teeth" (Matthew 13:49-50). God will separate the "wheat" from the "weeds," and the "good fish" from the "bad [fish]," and the "sheep" from the "goats" (Matthew 13:36-42, 47-48; 25:32). It is the "unrighteous [that] will not inherit the kingdom of God" (1 Corinthians 6:9).

When we hear about a planeload of people dying in a crash, without knowing any of them personally, we grieve. We think of their pain, the sorrow of their families. Suppose, however, that we know what young twelve-year-old Susan knows—that her father, the man in seat 23C, has been molesting her for two years and plans to do so that evening when he gets home. If we did know this, we might weep in relief that a *wicked* man is no longer alive to destroy an innocent young life. Our ability to sympathize or grieve over someone's death and judgment is largely guided by this judicial sentiment.

When we speak of God's wrath coming on *people* rather than on the *wicked*, we invariably sense a oneness with them rather than with God. But this puts us in opposition to God and the righteousness of his ways. Therefore, this difference in the language we use is important. We ought to take our cue from the moral and judicial language of Scripture; that God loves the *humble* but opposes the *proud* (James 4:6), that he honors the *tearful* (Isaiah 38:5) but warns the *obstinate* (Isaiah 30:1), and so forth. The judgments of the Lord are right, true, and truly praiseworthy. The people of God will rejoice when God brings an end to the *wicked*. This is not beyond our current judicial sentiment. Law-abiding, peace-loving people rejoice when the corrupt are judged and removed from power or the violent are judged and removed from the presence of the community. How much more will we say of the perfect Judge, "We give thanks to you, Lord God

Almighty. . . . for rewarding your servants, . . . and for destroying the destroyers of the earth" (Revelation 11:17-18).

In addition, it is simply not possible to square the idea that God does not send the wicked to hell—that they choose to go there—with either reason or Scripture.[7] It is the proper and reasonable role of all judges to execute punishment. This is not a passive role. When a man is sent to prison for his criminal behavior, he is *sent* there. He does not choose to go there. In the same way, when final judgment comes, God is active, not passive, in his role as the righteous Judge.

The wicked do not choose hell. It may be more accurate to say they choose to reject heaven. If we reject God and his supremacy, if we live to deface his glory, then heaven is the last place we would enjoy. But the wicked *never* choose hell. They go there against their will, "weeping and gnashing [their] teeth" (Matthew 25:30). In all of his judgment, God, boldly and without apology, takes an active role, not a passive one. In Revelation 19:2, final judgment is described as *God avenging* the shedding of innocent blood. In Matthew 10:28, final judgment is described as *God destroying* "both soul and body in hell." In Matthew 11:23, Jesus says the wicked are "brought down" to hell. The wicked do not leap or fall into the lake of fire. They are *thrown* into it, on purpose, according to the perfect righteousness of God. "And if anyone's name was not found written in the book of life, he was *thrown* into the lake of fire" (Revelation 20:15). Sobering, to be sure. May it also be motivating.

ACKNOWLEDGING OUR TRUE NEED FOR FORGIVENESS

All that is revealed about God's wrath has a loving purpose. In the revelation of God's wrath we become aware of the true nature of sin. We discover that our guilt is far, far greater than we ever felt. We acknowledge that God's judgment is just. We rightfully begin to despair that there is anything reparative that we can do in our own right to counterbalance the just penalty for sin. No amount of self-punishment can meet the just penalty for our rebellion. No effort at self-correction or meritorious works can counterbalance the weight of our sin. We are made aware that we have no answer to the question, "How are you to escape being sentenced to hell?" (Matthew 23:33). We simply and wonderfully are rendered aware of our need for grace and grace alone.

THE HUMAN EXPERIENCE OF GOD'S OUTWORKING GRACE

In the outworking of God's grace, there is a revelation of the wrath of God that leads to the discovery that our sin is far greater than we knew and that its wickedness is far worse than we thought. In the human experience of this grace, we acknowledge prayerfully the justice of God's judgment. "Against you, you only, have I sinned and done what is evil in your sight, so that you may be justified in your words and blameless in your judgment" (Psalm 51:4).

GROUP STUDY QUESTIONS

1. What has been the central drive of your life up to this point? According to Romans 1:18-23, what is God's purpose for your life?
2. According to Romans 1:18-23, why is God *right* to be angry with us? What evil do we commit *against God* whenever we sin, however we sin?
3. What is the point of the silly story of working for the White House cat?
4. How have I traced out the "exceeding sinfulness of sin" in my account of the stolen hat? Why do I argue that Romans 14:23 is the most "shocking truth" in the Bible?
5. Before reading this chapter, what were your impressions of God's wrath, final judgment, and hell? How has your understanding changed in light of the biblical testimony?
6. Is God's judgment too severe, or are we worse sinners than we thought?
7. According to Romans 2:8, what is it that we are truly repenting *from* when we repent? What are we repenting *to* in repentance? How should the day *after* we repent be different from the day *before* we repent?

4

THE GREAT WORK PROMISED

Putting Our Hope in God

I feel my shame inside me like a knife.
He told me I had a soul.
How does he know?
What spirit comes to move my life?
Is there another way to go?
—JEAN VALJEAN, IN *LES MISÉRABLES*

But the LORD *takes pleasure in those who fear him,*
in those who hope in his steadfast love.
—PSALM 147:11

Charles Simeon (1758–1836) wrote, "The truth is not in the middle and not in one extreme, but in both extremes."[1] An example of this is found in Romans 11:22: "Note then the kindness and the severity of God." God's response to our guilt is not somewhere between wrath and kindness, and it is not one or the other. His response is extreme wrath *and* extreme kindness.

In the previous chapter we looked at the severity of God's wrath. We turn now to consider the extremity of God's kindness and to ask, if God has shown us his wrath, and exposed our rebellion, and grieved us over our sin, to what purpose did he do this? Is it not to spare us? If so, what hope is there that God can forgive? How can he do so without making a mockery of his own righteousness? Under what conditions does he forgive? What we will see is that without devaluing God's justice, God's loving-kindness is *at work* to bring forgiveness and freedom to all who turn from their own way and put their hope in his unfailing love.

ANOREXIA OF THE SOUL

This hope is not wishful thinking nor mere optimism. In truth it is born out of a deep and genuine conviction of the awfulness of our actions. The biblical phrase for this is "godly grief." Its counterpart is despair, or "worldly grief." They are similar in that they both inflict pain and anguish over selfish and sinful behavior. The difference is that one leads to repentance and renewal while the other leads to hopelessness and death. Second Corinthians 7:10 says, *"Godly* grief produces a repentance that leads to salvation without regret, whereas *worldly* grief produces death."

How is it that one kind of grief is good for us and the other is bad, even deadly? In another context, this time dealing with the sorrow that comes from the death of loved ones, Paul gives us a clue about the crucial difference: "We do not want you to be uninformed, brothers, about those who are asleep, that you may not grieve as others do who have no hope" (1 Thessalonians 4:13). Worldly grief is grief *with no hope in it.* This is a solid definition of despair. Once we are finally convinced that we need God's forgiveness, we can become firmly convinced that we can never obtain it. We leap from denial right into despair. But ongoing, immovable despair under the conviction of sin and guilt leads to death. It is an anorexia of the soul.

An anorexic is firmly convinced (deceived, really) that eating food, the very source of life, is bad for her and will make her worse than she already is. Even as she starves herself, shrinking to skin and bones, she loathes eating. Without intervention, this sickness leads to death.

Despair works like anorexia—but in a soul. We slowly starve ourselves to death because the very source of nourishment, the God of
abundant life, has become, in our mind's eye, poison. Søren
Kierkegaard even titled his book on despair *The Sickness unto Death*,
concluding, "The despairing man is mortally ill."[2] He is echoing
Paul's warning that worldly grief produces death.

In contrast, godly grief is godly precisely because God is *working*
his good purposes through it. It is God-inflicted grief for a God-
glorifying reason. God-inflicted sorrow, no matter how painful, is not
deadly because the tears are leavened with hope. They are tears
brought to God. We grieve over what we have done, but we grieve
before God. Our shame causes us to turn to God in repentant faith,
rather than run from God into further dissipation and ruin. Godly
grief weeps, but because it also hopes, these tears eventually lead us
to salvation. "Godly grief produces a repentance that leads to *salvation* without regret."

FRANK AT THE CROSSROADS OF HOPE AND DESPAIR

Frank describes himself as a "lapsed" Catholic. "The more I lived in
the world," he told me, "the more irrelevant and unreal Christianity
became. After I studied literary criticism in college, I lost hope that the
Bible could be relied upon as a guide to know God. Now I'm not sure
what to believe or whom to believe."

Frank was at a point in his life where he wanted to find the truth
and relevance of his childhood faith. I suggested he take a childlike
approach. "Ask God to teach you, and read his Word with a teach-
able heart." After that we stayed in touch through e-mail. In one of
my notes I wrote:

> Frank, we read in Psalm 147:11, "The LORD takes pleasure in those
> who fear him, in those who *hope* in his steadfast love." Clearly the
> Lord does not hold a grudge. He could play "hard to get" when we
> finally call out to him. Instead, when he sees us turn with a search-
> ing heart, no matter how confused we are or what our starting point
> is, he experiences great delight in this one thing: we have *turned to*

him for some instruction, with a sense of dependence on him (hope). Clearly he delights in our hope in him.

Frank e-mailed me back the next day:

> Thank you for the encouragement. I have tried to put the thoughts I have had in the past (such as: "it is too late"; "too much has happened"; "why should he?" etc.) out of my head, and approach God honestly: as one who knows his past was not always correct, who wants to correct it.

Frank confirmed how common it is for people to get bogged down in despair once they sense the sinfulness of unbelief. In *Pilgrim's Progress,* John Bunyan's allegorical outline of Christian experience, the first obstacle the young Pilgrim encounters as he starts his journey toward the Celestial City is the "Slough of Despond." Frank's letter showed me that he had arrived at this sticky point. A spark of desire within and a growing conviction regarding his unfaithfulness compelled him to look toward God. But the same burden tempted him to ask, "Is there any realistic hope for me?" Like Frank, we all tend to leap from denial to despair because we can see *no way* for God to forgive without making a mockery of his holiness and justice. But since both denial and despair lead to death, the only way to pass through this painful season of regret and sorrow is to put our hope in God.

BIBLICAL HOPE IS NOT FOR UNIVERSAL FORGIVENESS

In putting our hope in God, we are not hoping that God will forgive us simply because he must. Biblical hope is fully cognizant that God does not forgive everyone. It does not say, "Ah, God is loving. He must forgive everyone." No such God is found in Scripture. Biblical hope trusts in the true and sovereign God, who has declared, "I will be gracious to whom I will be gracious, and will show mercy on whom I will show mercy" (Exodus 33:19). This is God's claim to fame; he alone is sovereign. He has an absolutely free will. This, God declares, is what makes him God!

> Our God is in the heavens;
> he does all that he pleases (Psalm 115:3).

His sovereignty includes the right to give his mercy to some without being obligated to give it to all.

For example, God did forgive Noah but not the people of Noah's day:

> The LORD saw that the wickedness of man was great in the earth, and that every intention of the thoughts of his heart was only evil continually. . . . The LORD said, "I will blot out man whom I have created from the face of the land, man and animals and creeping things and birds of the heavens, for I am sorry that I have made them." But Noah found favor in the eyes of the LORD (Genesis 6:5, 7-8).

Noah's generation grew so wicked that God wiped it out. Noah and his family received grace; the others got what their wickedness deserved.

God did not forgive the morally bankrupt people of Sodom and Gomorrah. Their sense of moral decency had sunk so low that it was permissible for a group of men to attempt to gang-rape two male visitors to their town. What they did not know was that the two men were servants of God (angels) sent to Lot to warn him to flee the coming judgment. God had endured enough. The horrific intentions against the servants confirmed just how horrible the people's rebellion and wickedness had grown. The two servants said to Lot,

> For we are about to destroy this place, because the outcry against its people has become great before the LORD, and the LORD has sent us to destroy it. . . . Up! Take your wife and your two daughters who are here, lest you be swept away in the punishment of the city (Genesis 19:13, 15).

Lot experienced God's kindness (19:16, 19). As for the rest, "The LORD rained on Sodom and Gomorrah sulfur and fire from the LORD out of heaven" (19:24).

Pharaoh is another example of someone God did not forgive. "Let my people go!" God commanded. Pharaoh clenched his fist and defied God. "Who is the LORD, that I should obey his voice . . . ? I do not know the LORD, and moreover, I will not let Israel go" (Exodus 5:2). God separated the sea for the people of Israel to escape the rushing army of Pharaoh. When Pharaoh and his men pursued them, the sea swept in and destroyed them all. In Exodus 14:18 God said, "The Egyptians shall know that I am the LORD, when I have gotten glory over Pharaoh, his chariots, and his horsemen." God gained glory in their destruction.

Joshua led Israel into the Promised Land with a severe warning: "He is a holy God. He is a jealous God; *he will not forgive your transgressions or your sins.* If you forsake the LORD and serve foreign gods, then he will turn and do you harm and consume you, after having done you good" (Joshua 24:19-20). This was a severe promise, a warning not to presume upon God's grace. He is under no obligation to forgive.

Joshua's warning came to pass in the days of Manasseh, king of Judah. The people's rebellion against the will of God reached its zenith when they turned to the ultimate act of divine contempt: sacrificing precious children to false gods (2 Chronicles 33:6).[3] God took away the Promised Land from the people he had promised it to, because they had broken the conditions of the promise (abiding faith). He handed the land over to the king of Babylon, who killed many and exiled the rest. Lest we doubt that this was God's doing, 2 Kings 24:3-4 says:

> Surely this came upon Judah *at the command of the LORD,* to remove them out of his sight, for the sins of Manasseh, according to all that he had done, and also for the innocent blood that he had shed. For he filled Jerusalem with innocent blood, *and the LORD* would not pardon.

The leaders of Israel who failed to defend the weak and rescue the poor were not forgiven (Jeremiah 5:27-29). Jesus warned the Pharisees that God would not forgive them for their self-righteousness and hypocrisy (Luke 11:42-52). Judas was not forgiven (Acts 1:25). Our hope in God clearly recognizes that God does not forgive everyone. He is under no obligation to forgive the wicked. Therefore, it is appropriate that we should wrestle under the conviction of our guilt with the question, "What hope is there for me?" It is a life-changing question if we hang with it long enough to find the answer.

WHAT HAPPENED WHEN JOHN NEWTON PUT HIS HOPE IN GOD

On March 9, 1748, John Newton (1725–1807) was in the midst of a violent storm at sea. Gigantic waves pounded and thrashed his ship, *The Greyhound*. One side of the ship was so battered and the water was rushing in so fast that the men despaired of their lives. All hands were preparing to die, including Newton. He was only twenty-three years old.

Newton had been raised by a godly mother who died when he was seven. His exposure to any earnest Christian faith ended there. At eleven John's father took him to sea. By the time he was twenty-three and sailing into the storm, he had a wide, well-founded reputation for being lazy, lustful, rebellious, and crude. He despised the "weakness" of Christians and loved to destroy the faith of any sailors who came on board. He prided himself in being the instigator of everything obscene. He wrote, "My life was one of continual godlessness and profanity. I do not know that I ever met a man with a mouth more vile than my own." Looking back on his youth, Newton later wrote, "Not only did I sin, but I got others to sin with me."[4]

The ship captain was especially offended by Newton's crude and blasphemous jokes against the Christian faith. When the storm hit, the captain cursed Newton as a "Jonah." The other sailors would have gladly thrown him overboard except that Newton was manning the pumps on that ferocious night at sea. The captain knew that if he could not turn the ship around to ease the stress on the battered side, they would sink with the next gigantic wave. According to Peter Masters's biographical sketch of Newton,

> [Newton] turned to look at the flooded area of the ship which he had been pumping. "If that won't do," he said, "the Lord have mercy on us." Suddenly, for the first time in years, his blasphemous words seemed to bite back at him. "What mercy do I deserve?" he thought. The answer seemed painfully obvious.

The color drained from his face and his mocking, arrogant manner gave way to deep fear and clamoring thoughts. . . . How could he face the God whom he had insulted for so long? He began to feel a crushing despair.[5]

The ship did not sink. The calm returned. But God had stirred up an inward storm. In the privacy of his quarters Newton read the Bible, searching to understand what hope he might have for obtaining God's forgiveness. Godly sorrow was producing true repentance.

To zoom forward, John Newton lived eighty-two years and became an oak tree of righteousness. He developed a passion for the worship of God, as his hymn "Amazing Grace" testifies. He became a man of the Book and a herald of the good news of the gospel. He was ordained in the Anglican Church, preaching and testifying for decades. He became a man of compassion—personally supporting and caring for the poet William Cowper through his many years of mental illness and suicide attempts. Newton became a man of moral courage in confronting public injustice as well.

In his seafaring days, Newton had sailed on slave ships, even becoming the captain of one, where he saw firsthand the inhumanity of that wretched traffic. Years later he wrote a book denouncing the slave trade to help William Wilberforce, a member of Parliament, in his crusade to abolish it in England.

Newton is a testimony to all that grace can accomplish as it works itself out over a lifetime. Newton's admission about his own early life could have led to hopeless despair and eternal death. Instead he turned to God in sorrow over his sin. This led to a repentance that transformed his whole life and changed the world forever.

GOD HAS A HEART TO FORGIVE

God has made it abundantly clear that, while he does not forgive everyone, he has a heart to forgive. If we could see God, we would see that he is by nature a God of loving-kindness who is able to forgive great wickedness. We know this because Moses once asked to see God (Exodus 33:18), and God said, "Fine":

The LORD passed before him and proclaimed, "The LORD, the LORD, a God merciful and gracious, slow to anger, and abounding in steadfast love and faithfulness, keeping steadfast love for thousands, forgiving iniquity and transgression and sin, but who will by no means clear the guilty, visiting the iniquity of the fathers on the children and the children's children, to the third and the fourth generation" (Exodus 34:6-7).

We have yet to answer *how* God punishes the guilty and yet forgives the wickedness of thousands, but we are coming to that. First we must see that he has a heart to do it. The Lord *is* gracious. The Lord *is* abounding in love. He *is* willing to forgive wickedness, rebellion, and sin.

GOD'S JUDGMENT COMES ONLY AS A LAST RESORT

God is slow to anger. His punishment comes as a *last* resort after *many* warnings. In Noah's day God saw that mankind's rebellion and depravity had grown to full maturity, "that every intention of the thoughts of his heart was only evil continually" (Genesis 6:5). God's judgment did not come when the people first sinned or even when their wickedness grew to full maturity. He endured 120 more years of their all-pervasive wickedness, warning them throughout those years to repent, before he finally said, "Enough" (6:3). Even as Noah banged away on the ark, he warned them to turn their hearts to God. When they did not repent, the floodgates were released.

God did not forgive Pharaoh, but remember, for *four hundred years* the Israelites suffered oppression by the Egyptians (see Genesis 15:13). God heard their cries and was concerned about their suffering (Exodus 3:7). They had to suffer long because God is long-suffering with the wicked. Even when he finally came to judge Egypt and deliver Israel, he approached Pharaoh more than *ten times* before his wrath was finally unleashed.

Judas's hypocrisy was patiently endured by Jesus for three years, and not just any three years. Judas saw Jesus healing the blind and raising the dead. He heard the kingdom of God proclaimed. What about God's judgment on the Pharisees and the other leaders of Jerusalem? Jesus wept over Jerusalem (Luke 19:41). Their hardness of heart meant they would not know the forgiveness of God, though he was inclined to give it.

God prefers mercy over judgment: "As I live, declares the Lord GOD, I have no pleasure in the death of the wicked, but that the wicked turn from his way and live; turn back, turn back from your evil ways, for why will you die, O house of Israel?" (Ezekiel 33:11). This is the heart of God:

> . . . though he cause grief, he will have compassion
>   according to the abundance of his steadfast love;
> for he does not willingly afflict
>   or grieve the children of men (Lamentations 3:32-33).

Daniel Fuller calls judgment the penultimate (next-to-last) desire of God's heart:

> We may sum up the relationship between God's love and wrath with the statement, so vital for understanding his plan in redemptive history, that God's kindness . . . is his free, ultimate work in which his soul finally and fully delights, whereas God's wrath in punishment is his necessary, penultimate work. Though he finds no pleasure in punishing the wicked, he nevertheless does it as something he must do, so that without devaluing his glory, he can fully rejoice in being merciful to the penitent.[6]

WILLING TWO THINGS AT ONCE

I recently served on a trial jury. The man on trial had been caught selling crack cocaine. He had a "domestic partner" and a couple of children. But he was a drug dealer, and many mothers in the tenement feared for the well-being of their children. When I looked at the man's "wife," I felt sad for her. I thought of his small children and wondered what was going to happen to this poor family now. It troubled me to do my duty and render a just and correct verdict, though he was truly guilty according to the evidence. I grieved that I had to convict him and send him to jail. In this sense, God also grieves. He does not delight in punishment per se.

But there was more to look at than just the man and his family. I looked at the housing project he lived in, and the many poor families desperately crying out for city leaders to remove drugs and dealers from their area. Poor mothers love their children and desire their protection just as much as more wealthy mothers do. I thought of the pain they would bear if I let him go. I could anticipate their joy should he be removed from their lives. So I could feel pain and pleasure at the same time, depending on my focus.

God's emotions have a similarly bifocal quality. He can say, "For I have *no pleasure* in the death of anyone" (Ezekiel 18:32). But elsewhere we read, "the LORD will take *delight* in bringing ruin upon you and destroying you" (Deuteronomy 28:63). Clearly God can grieve for one reason (love for his creation) over something that he does (judgment) that for another reason (love for his name and his people) he delights to do.

WHOM DOES GOD FORGIVE?

Whom does God forgive and under what conditions does he forgive? God forgives those who put their hope in him—the very God who condemns them for their wickedness:

> . . . the LORD takes pleasure in those who fear him,
>   in those who hope in his steadfast love (Psalm 147:11).

What is it that we are doing when we put our hope in God? We are putting our hope in God when we *trust* in the Lord (Psalm 32:10); *humble* ourselves before the Lord (Proverbs 3:34); *wait* for the Lord (Isaiah 30:18); *fear* the Lord (Psalm 31:19); *love* the Lord (Exodus 20:5-6); *turn* to the Lord (Isaiah 55:7); *take refuge* in the Lord (Psalm 31:19); *seek* the Lord (Psalm 34:10); *repent* (Isaiah 59:20); and *have faith* in the Lord (2 Chronicles 20:20). Those who do these things are the objects of God's loving-kindness:

> Behold, the eye of the LORD is on those who *fear* him,
>   on those who *hope* in his steadfast love,

that he may deliver their soul from death . . .
Our soul *waits* for the LORD;
   he is our help and our shield.
For our heart is glad in him,
   because we *trust* in his holy name.
Let your steadfast love, O LORD, be upon us,
   even as *we hope in you* (Psalm 33:18-22).

Whom does God forgive? In 2 Chronicles 30:9 the answer is, "The LORD your God is *gracious and merciful* and will not turn away his face from you, *if you return to him.*" In Psalm 86:5 the answer is, "For you, O Lord, are good and forgiving, abounding in steadfast love to all who *call upon you.*"

Clearly it is not simply *sinning* that damns us. It is sinning *and not repenting.* Despair is appropriate only for the unrepentant and obstinate who refuse to turn their hearts toward God. Romans 2:5 says, "But because of your hard and *impenitent* heart you are storing up wrath for yourself on the day of wrath when God's righteous judgment will be revealed." Contrast this with Joel 2:12-13:

"Yet even now," declares the LORD,
   "return to me with all your heart,
with fasting, with weeping, and with mourning;
   and rend your hearts and not your garments."
Return to the LORD, your God,
   for he is gracious and merciful,
slow to anger, and abounding in steadfast love;
   and he relents over disaster.

This is a clarion, pleading call from God for us to turn from sin and to put our hope in him. To personalize it, this means that I look to God's loving-kindness and trust that, while he is right to be angry and is just to condemn me, his kindness is so extraordinary that he himself will make a way for his forgiveness to flow to me and restore our broken relationship. I may not yet understand how God can show me mercy without devaluing his justice, but I trust that God does have a plan to accomplish this very thing.

GOD HAS A MIRACLE PLANNED

When we put our hope in God, we are really waiting and watching for God *to provide a miracle on our behalf*. To hope means to trust that God has a plan to execute his punishment against us and extend his pardon to us at the same time. This very plan was first revealed to Abraham. God told Abraham, "Take your son, your only son Isaac, whom you love, and go to the land of *Moriah,* and offer him there as a burnt offering on one of the mountains of which I shall tell you" (Genesis 22:2). Abraham obeyed. Why did God command Abraham to do this? First, to test the substance of his faith, whether it was full of trust and dependence and obedience, or whether it was a worthless and false faith (22:1, 12). But second, to teach Abraham and all who came after him that God had a plan to provide a substitute punishment for sin. When Abraham had the knife ready, God called him to stop, commended him for his obedient faith, and then pointed out the lesson:

> And Abraham lifted up his eyes and looked, and behold, behind him was a ram, caught in a thicket by his horns. And Abraham went and took the ram and offered it up as a burnt offering instead of his son. So Abraham called the name of that place, "The LORD will provide"; as it is said to this day, "On the mount of the LORD it shall be provided" (22:13-14).

Abraham learned and trusted—"On the mountain of the Lord it will be provided." Mount Moriah is not mentioned again until the days of King Solomon. Then, lo and behold, "Solomon began to build the house of the LORD in Jerusalem on Mount *Moriah*" (2 Chronicles 3:1). Where? On Mount Moriah in Jerusalem. Abraham's mountain! Centuries after Abraham first learned that God would provide a substitute on this mountain, the temple was built there, and for centuries to come countless animal sacrifices would be made on Mount Moriah, daily reminding the people that a substitute punishment for sin was needed and would be provided one day by God.

When that day came, God led his Son, his only Son, his beloved Son to the very same spot. Matthew 16:21 says, "Jesus began to show his disciples that he *must go to Jerusalem* and suffer many things from the elders and chief priests and scribes, and be killed, and on the third day be raised." Why Jerusalem? Because God promised those who hope in him that *on the mountain of the Lord it would be provided*. I doubt that Abraham ever fully understood why he was commanded to take his son up the mountain as an offering. That is for us to savor as we turn now to the gospel of Jesus Christ—the gift of God.

THE HUMAN EXPERIENCE OF GOD'S OUTWORKING GRACE

Having grieved us over our sin, God works to draw us to his loving-kindness. We experience this grace as putting our hope in God and trusting that he has a way planned to forgive our sins and restore our broken relationship with him, without devaluing his righteousness.

GROUP STUDY QUESTIONS

1. Why is despair so dangerous, even deadly? What does despair make us do? According to 2 Corinthians 7:10, what is the difference between godly sorrow and worldly sorrow? Which experience are you more familiar with?

2. Many people believe God's love requires him to forgive everybody, including those who do not believe in or even acknowledge him. How do we know this is not true? Why can we be certain that God has a heart to forgive?

3. How is it that God can will two things at once? For example, how can he both delight to punish and grieve to punish? How have I illustrated that we also have this same capacity?

4. What is the alternative to denying our sin or despairing over our sin? According to Psalm 147:11, what is God's response to us when we make him "our hope"? What does it mean to "put your hope in God"?

5. Reading Genesis 22, how can you tell that Abraham put his hope in God? What did he learn by taking his only son up Mount Moriah? What central promise of God are we depending on when we put our hope in God? Why are we "hoping for a miracle" when we hope in God?

5

THE GREAT WORK
REVEALED

Discovering Christ as Rescuer

It is unworthy of God to unite himself to wretched man, yet it is not unworthy of God to lift man up out of his wretchedness.
—BLAISE PASCAL, *PENSÉES*

[God] has delivered us from the domain of darkness and transferred us to the kingdom of his beloved Son, in whom we have redemption, the forgiveness of sins.
—COLOSSIANS 1:13-14

Magalie was illegally brought from Haiti to Boston by her father, through Canada, when she was thirteen years old. She graduated from high school five years later. Then her father abandoned her to take up with his new wife. When my staff and I met Magalie, she had no place to live and no means of support. Because she was an illegal alien, she could not get a job—and she was pregnant by a man who did not want to provide for her and their child. Desperate, she considered abortion, then decided to kill herself. We were able to intervene and help her. Seven months later, she gave birth to a beautiful son.

I could not get her a job, though, because obtaining a green card, the legal permit to work, is a long and expensive process. A "friend" offered to help Magalie obtain working papers for five hundred dollars. She borrowed the money, paid him, and signed the papers he prepared for her. At the court hearing, the judge asked Magalie a series of questions based on those documents. She immediately realized that the man who had taken her money had falsified the entire story of her life to get her "political asylum." She did not want to lie to the judge, and since she could not validate her claim for political asylum, he immediately set a deportation hearing date.

In tears, Magalie called me and asked if I would go with her to her deportation hearing, since she could not afford a lawyer. I had her sit down and write the true story of her life. I had her "agree with her accuser" that she had misled the court by signing false statements. I had her ask the court to help her understand what the right and proper steps were for obtaining working papers in this country, with the pledge that she would work hard to provide for herself and her son if given a chance. To this I added my own letter.

Into the courtroom we walked. We sat before the bench, staring at the seal of the United States government. The judge sat above us in his formal black robe. Microphones and recorders noted every word spoken "for the record." Magalie trembled in her seat. The judge spoke deliberately and asked long, memorized questions. With each answer Magalie drew one step closer to expulsion. Magalie cut him off by confessing that the document before him was false and that she had written her true story and would like to submit it to him. The judge stopped the proceedings and went "off the record" to read over her story and my accompanying letter.

I saw before me a judge who was used to being lied to, not confessed to. I had witnessed him setting deportation dates for the two cases heard before Magalie's. He impressed me as a man governed by a sense of integrity and justice. Although principled, he was not cold-hearted. He was willing to let Magalie say what she had to say, no matter how broken her English or meandering her explanation. He read my letter too. I held my breath and prayed. How could justice and mercy *both* be upheld?

The judge swung into action. He gave Magalie a number of new forms and ordered her to fill them out and return them to him. *Grace!* I thought to myself. He advised her—no, he *urged* her—to get a lawyer to oversee the process. Magalie confessed that she had no money for a lawyer and that several pro bono places had turned down her case already (probably because of the fraudulent documents). Magalie could not save herself, even with the court's instructions and patience. The judge shook his head in frustration. He was clearly considering what more, if anything, he was willing to do.

Suddenly he turned to the clerk and instructed her to go immediately to his office and retrieve the phone number of a *personal* friend of his. Then he turned to Magalie. "Call him and tell him *I* told you to call," said the judge. "He will help you." Then he told her plainly that if she failed to call this man and follow his instructions and return to the bench with the properly filled out papers, he would summarily deport her.

The judge wanted to show kindness to Magalie. But to ensure that it would not compromise the law (and therefore his integrity as one sworn to uphold it) he sent his own personal friend to help bring Magalie into conformity with the law. *He was working to win her the right to live here lawfully.* For the first time, I could envision Magalie going to work every day and making a quiet life for herself and her son without fear. The judge was as aware as I of how gracious his help was. If she rejected it, he would rightly have applied the law without mercy and deported her.

I sat there deeply moved, muttering to myself, "Behold the kindness and sternness of the judge," but I was thinking of God, really. As lawbreakers, we stand before him who is sworn to uphold his righteousness. God's instructions on keeping the law are not enough. We lack the means to bring ourselves into compliance. But because of his loving-kindness, God made a way for his mercy to be *justly* given to sinners who would otherwise deserve eternal deportation from his kingdom. He sent his own Son to do the work that we could not do, to meet the just requirements of the law; and he did so pro bono, free of charge.

YES AND AMEN

So far we have stressed that, though God makes us aware of our guilt and of the rightness of his judgment, he nonetheless calls us to put our hope in him. He calls us to trust him to acquit us, *somehow*. I say somehow, because we are mindful that God cannot acquit the guilty any more than he can condemn the innocent and be true to himself as a holy and righteous God. Now we turn to discover God's response to the hopeful.

We discover that in putting our hope in God, we are called to put our trust in Jesus. In the outworking of God's grace, Jesus is the miracle we were hoping for. Jesus is the meaning of the promise, "The LORD will provide" (Genesis 22:14). Through Jesus, God determined to reveal his mercy and to justify his grace. This is evident right from the beginning of the gospel story. The angel of the Lord instructed Mary about the miracle in her womb, "You shall call his name *Jesus,* for he will *save* his people from their sins" (Matthew 1:21). The name Jesus literally means "Rescuer" or "Savior."

From the four portraits of Jesus in the Gospels we can summarize his rescue mission as accomplishing two great things at once: he is fulfilling all of God's promises to pardon, reconcile, and transform our lives so that we can live a life pleasing to him; and he is fulfilling all our hopes for an unburdened conscience, freedom from habitual sin, and an unbridled joy and confidence in God. Put together, Jesus is the fulfillment of all of God's glorious promises to us who put our hope in him. Notice how the two come together in 2 Corinthians 1:20: "For all the promises of God find their *Yes* in him. That is why it is through him that we utter our *Amen* to God for his glory." Through Jesus, God says *yes* to all his promises and we shout *amen* for our newly redeemed lives. Jesus is the God-sent miracle we are hoping for when we put our hope in God.

MIRACLE AND MYSTERY IN JESUS

The first glimpses we get of Jesus as our great Rescuer come from the Old Testament prophecies about him.[1] Abraham learned that a substitute would be provided (Genesis 22:14). He and the generations of

Israel that followed were taught to wait in hope. The first clear description of Jesus as the fulfillment of God's promise to provide came centuries later. Isaiah was told, "The virgin shall conceive and bear a son, and shall call his name Immanuel" (7:14). Immanuel means "God with us." Here is the clearest expression of the miracle and the mystery of the incarnation. I say miracle because God promised to send this child "born of a virgin." And I say mystery because he was God with *us;* God in the flesh. "He is the *image* of the *invisible* God" (Colossians 1:15). When God thinks of himself or speaks of himself in all his perfections and excellencies, the word that emerges is Jesus. "In the beginning was the Word, and the Word was with God, and the Word was God. . . . And the Word became flesh and dwelt among us" (John 1:1, 14).

Isaiah 9:6 adds a few more details about the miracle and mystery of the incarnation:

> For to us a child is born,
> to us a son is given;
> and the government shall be upon his shoulder,
> and his name shall be called
> Wonderful Counselor, Mighty God,
> Everlasting Father, Prince of Peace.

A *son* is given, yet he is called the *Everlasting Father?* A *child* is born, yet he is called *Mighty God?* Mysterious? Infinitely so. Miraculous? To be sure. Surprising? Wondrously surprising. The Jews called him Messiah, or anointed one (John 1:41; see also Daniel 9:25). He was also called the Redeemer (Isaiah 59:20) and the *hope* of Israel (Jeremiah 14:8). When God was ready to reward hope with fulfillment, he came to our rescue in the form of a child, and that child was named Jesus. His name was Jesus because he came to rescue every repentant sinner, all who put their hope in God.[2]

A few people, and only a few, were able to recognize in the birth of Christ the promised Savior described by Isaiah centuries before. Mary and Joseph knew this from the miraculous conception and from the angelic announcements surrounding Christ's birth (Matthew

1:20). Simeon, a man who prayerfully studied all the messianic prophecies, and Anna, a woman devoted to God, recognized who Jesus was from his infancy (Luke 2:25-38). But God, in his wisdom, let the revelation of Jesus as our Rescuer unfold slowly. Jesus grew up, learning obedience, maturing, and gaining a self-understanding of his mission in quiet obscurity.

BEFRIENDING THE "SINNERS"

When Jesus was thirty years old, he "went public." He was publicly commissioned through a baptismal service (Luke 3:21-23). From that point he started to reveal his nature and purpose in the world as our Rescuer. On one occasion, he used the prejudices of the culture to reveal who it was he had come to save:

> And as he reclined at table in his house, many tax collectors and sin-ners were reclining with Jesus and his disciples, for there were many who followed him. And the scribes of the Pharisees, when they saw that he was eating with sinners and tax collectors, said to his disci-ples, "Why does he eat with tax collectors and *sinners?*" And when Jesus heard it, he said to them, "Those who are well have no need of a physician, but those who are sick. I came not to call the righ-teous, but *sinners*" (Mark 2:15-17).

Both the Pharisees and Jesus use the word *sinner,* but in slightly different ways. The use in either case is jarring to the modern ear, so highly trained are we never to think negatively of ourselves. Hopefully we are past that obstacle by now. Not only are we not offended by it, we are glad to number ourselves among the sinners. It means that Jesus has us in view in the rescuing work that he came to do. When he says he did not come to *call the righteous,* he means that he did not come to bring the *self*-righteous into the grace and mercy of God. They admit to no wrongdoing that needs the cure of mercy. And when he says that he came to call sinners, he means he came to deliver *self-confessing* sinners into the grace of God.

But how are the Pharisees using the word *sinner?* To them it is a slur. Socially and economically (and racially), people incline to associate with those who are similar to them; rich and poor, educated and uneducated, Jew and Gentile, black and white, us and them. We look down at "them," using derogatory names. This is the sense in which the Pharisees use the word *sinner*. They mean the socially poor, the rabble, those who have no standing with God *as the scribes believed themselves to have*. Morally and spiritually we are all poor, uneducated, screwed up, and dysfunctional. This is Jesus' point. He goes to the socially poor to demonstrate that his mission is to rescue the spiritually poor.

I once had an interesting social experience that reminded me of this account. When I met Robert, he was "thirty-three years old going on fifty" due to a long history of drug and alcohol abuse. He was a huge man from the Deep South, who spoke atrocious English, worked multiple odd jobs, and owned nothing. He was stuck in Boston's worst neighborhood, lived on disability money, and had a sad and long story.

Robert and his girlfriend, Belinda, came to see our staff counselor and me every week for a time. I had been sowing a vision into Robert of being a husband and father and hard worker who loves and provides for his family. After all, he and Belinda had been together for seven years and she was having their first baby. On their third visit I learned that they were married, but each to *someone else*. Neither had seen his or her spouse in over ten years. None of the people involved had bothered to file for divorce.

In addition, Robert could not even read his own name. He "knows his numbers pretty good," he said to me, but not his letters. Where could I begin to sort this out? No money, no home, no job, no driver's license, newly sober (but would it last?), a baby on the way, a family to set up (but how?). Robert was a poor, messed-up, lost soul. He told me that since he couldn't read it, he slept with his Bible under his pillow every night as a way of showing God he wanted to do right.

One week I drove Belinda over to a Christian home for expectant mothers, then I took Robert out for Chinese food. You should have seen the businessmen turn their heads when I walked in with Robert in dreadlocks and shabby clothes. I was dressed in a white shirt and tie that day, and I could tell by the furtive looks that the lunch crowd was thinking, *Catch a load of these two together!* We sat there for an hour enjoying hot and sour soup, practicing our letters, sounding out words, and talking about Jesus. I drove home happy that day, thinking, *Jesus would have enjoyed eating Chinese food with Robert. Robert is a lost sinner and he knows it.* But more to the point, spiritually, *we are all Robert.* And in Jesus we have someone willing to take an interest in us. We have someone willing to take up our helpless cause and rescue us from a life of spiritual poverty and ruin.[3]

PARDONING THE "SINNERS"

Another discovery we make in surveying the life of Jesus in the Gospels is that he had the authority to forgive sinners. He is the Workman of God's outworking grace:

> And when he returned to Capernaum after some days, it was reported that he was at home. And many were gathered together, so that there was no more room, not even at the door. And he was preaching the word to them. And they came, bringing to him a paralytic carried by four men. And when they could not get near him because of the crowd, they removed the roof above him, and when they had made an opening, they let down the bed on which the paralytic lay. And when Jesus saw their faith, he said to the paralytic, *"My son, your sins are forgiven."*
>
> Now some of the scribes were sitting there, questioning in their hearts, "Why does this man speak like that? He is blaspheming! *Who can forgive sins but God alone?"*
>
> And immediately Jesus, perceiving in his spirit that they thus questioned within themselves, said to them, "Why do you question these things in your hearts? Which is easier, to say to the paralytic, 'Your sins are forgiven,' or to say, 'Rise, take up your bed and walk'? But that you may know that the Son of Man has authority on earth to forgive sins"—he said to the paralytic—"I say to you, rise, pick up your bed, and go home." And he rose and immediately picked up his bed and went out before them all, so that they were all amazed and glorified God, saying, "We never saw anything like this!" (Mark 2:1-12).

The disabled man leapt off his mat and started praising God while a bunch of religious professionals went ballistic. "Only *God* can forgive sins!" they protested. Jesus *agreed,* and that was, of course, the *point.* He was revealing that he had the fullness of God in himself; that included the authority to forgive sinners.

TRANSFORMING THE "SINNERS"

Jesus is called Savior because "he will save his people from their sins" (Matthew 1:21). Jesus is our great Rescuer because he rescues us from the penalty of our sins and from the enslaving power of sin. What a cruel joke it would be for God to forgive sinners and leave them habitually sinning. Blaise Pascal wrote in his famous *Pensées,* "It is unworthy of God to unite himself to wretched man, yet it is not unworthy of God to lift man up out of his wretchedness."[4] This is what Jesus does as our Rescuer. Jesus "saved us and called us to a holy calling" (2 Timothy 1:9). To get a true and accurate vision of Christ as our Rescuer, we must see that he rescues us from the heartfelt desire to habitually sin.

We see this in his commissioning of Paul as an apostle to the Gentiles: "I am sending you to open their eyes, so that they may turn from darkness to light and from the power of Satan to God, that they may receive forgiveness of sins and a place among those who are sanctified by faith in me" (Acts 26:17-18). The grace that prompts us to receive the forgiveness of sin goes on to prompt us to be sanctified. To be sanctified means to be made holy. Our Rescuer intends to transform our will-to-sin to a will-not-to-sin. Our rescue would be incomplete without this transformation. Our forgiveness would be subject to ridicule.

Jesus fully expects the life of God to be produced in those who hope for the forgiveness of God. In Luke 13:6-9 he teaches this by way of example:

> "A man had a fig tree planted in his vineyard, and he came seeking fruit on it and found none. And he said to the vinedresser, 'Look, for three years now I have come seeking fruit on this fig tree, and I find none. Cut it down. Why should it use up the ground?'

"And he answered him, 'Sir, let it alone this year also, until I dig around it and put on manure. Then if it should bear fruit next year, well and good; but if not, you can cut it down.'"

God is patient but nonetheless expecting to see the fruit that should come from heartfelt repentance and faith. If there is none, over a long period of time, then we too should question the sincerity of our repentance. But for those who have come to hate their sin and put their hope in God, we can trust that Jesus will not only earn a pardon for us but empower us to live a righteous life. This is another reason we call him our Rescuer.

IS JESUS THE ONLY WAY TO BE RESCUED?

"I and the Father are one" (John 10:30). What a remarkable claim! Jesus is asserting that his actions are representative of God's actions. He is the one Rescuer sent from God to forgive sinners. "I am the way, and the truth, and the life. No one comes to the Father except through me" (John 14:6). These striking claims drove the professional clergy nuts because they sounded so blasphemous and arrogant. Still today, the reaction is the same, but there it is. Jesus is the only way to be rescued from sin and death simply because he is the only miracle God sent into this world to be our Rescuer.

The rightness and reasonableness of Jesus making such exclusive claims on our faith can be illustrated (though admittedly imperfectly) by Magalie's experience before the judge. Imagine if Magalie had left the court and failed to call the lawyer provided personally by the judge. Here was the *one name* that the judge himself had provided. What if she had decided to go somewhere else? Would the judge's kindness be honored, or demeaned? Would he be angry or thrilled by her creative plan to get right with the law? He said he would deport her if she wavered or delayed in any way. He was willing to work her complete rescue, free of charge, but on one condition: she must trust him *by obeying his instructions.* The apostle Paul calls this "the obedience of faith" (Romans 1:5). Magalie expressed her faith in the judge by calling on *the* lawyer that the judge sent her to and by following his instructions.

So it is with us as we face deportation from God's kingdom. One lawyer has been sent and authorized to pardon our sins and bring us into compliance with the holy law of God. His name is Jesus. All roads do not lead to heaven; one way has been provided. There is no alternate route or plan B. The Jesus Plan rings well with God. "There is salvation in no one else, for there is no other name under heaven given among men by which we must be saved" (Acts 4:12). We try creative alternatives at our own peril.

A SPECIAL WORD TO THE HOPEFUL PLAGUED WITH DOUBTS

Still another discovery we make of Jesus is that no matter how sinful and guilty we are and feel, Jesus is equal to the task of rescuing and restoring us. In Luke 7:36-50 we read that a Pharisee named Simon had invited Jesus to dinner. Right in the middle of dinner a woman known in the town as a "sinful woman" barged in, carrying "an alabaster flask of ointment, and standing behind him at his feet, weeping, she began to wet his feet with her tears and wiped them with the hair of her head and kissed his feet and anointed them with the ointment" (7:37-38). Simon was shocked! "If this man were a prophet, he would have known who and what sort of woman this is who is touching him, for she is a sinner" (7:39).

What Simon failed to consider is that God has a heart for great sinners and accepts their confession and desire to be cleansed. He failed to consider that the greatness of God's mercy is revealed in showing mercy to great sinners! He failed to consider that if a small debt is forgiven, a small gratitude results, but if a great debt is forgiven, a greater heartfelt joy and thankfulness results. Jesus turned to his host and drove the point home:

> Then turning toward the woman [Jesus] said to Simon, "Do you see this woman? I entered your house; you gave me no water for my feet, but she has wet my feet with her tears and wiped them with her hair. You gave me no kiss, but from the time I came in she has not ceased to kiss my feet. You did not anoint my head with oil, but she has anointed my feet with ointment. Therefore I tell you, her sins,

which are many, are forgiven—for she loved much. But he who is forgiven little, loves little." And he said to her, "Your sins are forgiven" (Luke 7:44-48).

Great sinners make great lovers of God. Here is the confidence we need, if we are heavily burdened with shame and guilt. The question is not, "Can Christ forgive even me?" The question is how loud do you intend to shout God's praises, given all that he has forgiven you? Jesus welcomes and rewards repentant sinners who put their faith in him, no matter how deep and foul and embarrassing and shameful their past. "And he said to the woman, 'Your faith has saved you; go in peace'" (Luke 7:50).

JONATHAN EDWARDS'S EXCELLENT SAVIOR

There is much more we could say about the life and teaching of Jesus that reveals him to be our great Rescuer. It is important that we get to know him and continually discover how great a Savior he is—in fact, that continual discovery is the outworking of grace itself. The most winsome description of Jesus I have ever read comes from the famous American Puritan Jonathan Edwards in his sermon "The Excellency of Christ." He asks us to consider what we could ever want in a Savior that is not found in the person of Jesus Christ:

What is there that you can desire should be in a Savior, that is not in Christ? What excellency is there wanting? What is there that is great or good; what is there that is venerable or winning; what is there that is adorable or endearing; or what can you think of that would be encouraging, which is not to be found in the person of Christ?

Would you have your Savior to be great and honourable, because you are not willing to be beholden to a mean person? And is not Christ a person honourable enough to be worthy that you should be dependent on him; is he not a person high enough to be appointed to so honourable a work as your salvation? Would you not only have a Savior of high degree, but would you have him, notwithstanding his exaltation and dignity, to be made also of low degree, that he might have experience of afflictions and trials, that he might learn by the things that he has suffered, to pity them that suffer and are tempted? And has not Christ been made low enough for you; and has he not suffered enough?

Would you have your Savior to be one who is near to God, so that his mediation might be prevalent with him? And can you desire him to be nearer to God than Christ is, who is his only-begotten Son, of the same essence with the Father? And would you not only have him near to God, but also near to you, that you may have free access to him? And would you have him nearer to you than to be in the same nature, united to you by a spiritual union, so close as to be fitly represented by the union of the wife to the husband, of the branch to the vine, of the member to the head; yea, so as to be one spirit? For so he will be united to you, if you accept him. . . . What is there wanting or what would you add if you could, to make him more fit to be your Savior?[5]

Do you see how Edwards's discovery of the person and life of Jesus has produced a confident trust and genuine love for Jesus Christ? This is the path we must follow. We must learn about Jesus. As we do, we will discover how fit he is to be our Savior and how fitting it is that we should entrust ourselves to him. Through him our hopes are fulfilled and God's promises are kept. God rescues us through his appointed Rescuer, Jesus Christ. Or as Colossians 1:13-14 says, "[God] has delivered us from the domain of darkness and transferred us to the kingdom of his beloved Son, in whom we have redemption, the forgiveness of sins."

THE HUMAN EXPERIENCE OF GOD'S OUTWORKING GRACE

*God's promise to rescue and transform our lives, and our hope for a miracle,
find mutual fulfillment through the life and work of Jesus Christ.
He is the incarnation of the outworking of God's grace.
In the human experience of this outworking grace we move from putting
our hope in God to looking to Jesus as our true and excellent Savior.*

THE GREAT WORK OF THE GOSPEL
GROUP STUDY QUESTIONS

1. How familiar are you with the life and teaching of Jesus as recorded in the Gospels? If you have read one of the Gospels recently, what false perceptions did you have about Jesus, prior to reading, which changed as a result of reading his actual words and the accounts of his life?

2. How does Magalie's experience before the judge mirror the gospel story?

3. Why did Jesus come into the world, according to Mark 2:15-17? Who, then, are the only people Jesus cannot forgive?

4. In John 14:6, Jesus boldly claimed to be a "sinner's" *only* hope. Christian faith makes an exclusive claim to be the only way to experience God's forgiveness and reconciliation (Acts 4:12). Why is this so offensive to people in general? Why is the idea that all roads lead to heaven and that all religions are equally true and good, offensive to the God of the Bible?

5. At this point in your life, are you willing to express your hope in God as "faith in Jesus Christ"? Why or why not?

6

THE GREAT WORK
JUSTIFIED

Grasping the Truth of the Cross

Shame tears my soul, my body many a wound;
Sharp nails pierce this, but sharper that confound;
Reproaches, which are free, while I am bound;
Was ever grief like mine?
—GEORGE HERBERT, "THE SACRIFICE"

For our sake he made him to be sin who knew no sin, so that
in him we might become the righteousness of God.
—2 CORINTHIANS 5:21

Elie Wiesel is a Nobel Peace Prize recipient and a Jewish survivor of Auschwitz, the most horrific death camp of World War II. Dr. Wiesel's life mission has been to bring Nazi war criminals to the bar of justice and to remind the world of the immeasurable evil of the Holocaust. When Dr. Wiesel speaks, you can hear the wrenching cries of the innocent in his voice. He honors his people and all mankind by demanding justice and warning us, "Never again!"

On January 27, 1995, Dr. Wiesel joined other Jewish survivors of Auschwitz in a ceremony to pay tribute to Hitler's victims on the fiftieth anniversary of Auschwitz's "liberation" by the Russian army. As the group gathered around the remains of the concrete crematorium, Wiesel prayed, "God, merciful God, do not have mercy on murderers of Jewish children. Do not have mercy on those who created this place. Do not forgive the people who murdered here."[1]

How should God answer this prayer? To Dr. Wiesel, a merciful and just God must be able to get angry and punish, or he is neither merciful nor just. Dr. Wiesel is right. Justice demands that the murderers of millions of innocent Jewish children be cast into the hottest parts of hell's fire. But now the slope gets slippery. Once it is established that a just God cannot fail to punish the wicked, how will *anyone* escape? Even victims of sin are also perpetrators of sin, and the just wages of sin is death. In spite of this, we know that God has pardoned wicked sinners and we may assume that some of them are repentant murderers, even of children. How does God justify this? Nothing we have learned so far in our survey of the life of Jesus provides a sufficient answer. God would be wrong to pardon a Nazi war criminal, or any other sinner, including me, you, and Dr. Wiesel himself, based on what we have learned *so far* about the life of Christ.

God's answer to Dr. Wiesel and all of us caught in the pincers between a desire for mercy and a love of justice is the cross of Christ. Here mercy and justice kiss. Here God works to uphold his righteousness and to overflow with loving-kindness. Here God reconciles repentant sinners to himself. Here God is glorified and we are satisfied. To understand the outworking of God's forgiveness, we must soberly grasp the truth of the cross.

WHY DO WE CALL GOOD FRIDAY GOOD?

What happened in the death of Jesus Christ? Why is it good? At a key point in his ministry, Jesus took his twelve disciples aside and said,

> See, we are going up to Jerusalem, and everything that is written about the Son of Man by the prophets will be accomplished. For he will be delivered over to the Gentiles and will be mocked and shamefully treated and spit upon. And after flogging him, they will kill him, and on the third day he will rise (Luke 18:31-33).

The disciples did not get it. They could not conceive of a plan, a prophetic plan, in which the One they had pinned their hopes on was going to be murdered. They could not grasp any reason or benefit in such a crime. Here was a man feeding the hungry and teaching us how to love. Who would want to kill a miracle worker? Why would God allow it? In their mind, that would mean that the Rescuer needed rescuing. Jesus must have been mixed up. How could God *ordain*—that is, intentionally purpose—such a thing? God condemns the shedding of innocent blood (Deuteronomy 21:1-9). How could he then condone it when it comes to the most innocent of all men? On what basis could God *want* Jesus to be executed?

In spite of these solid arguments, events regarding Jesus happened just as Jesus predicted—and just as the prophet Isaiah had foretold centuries before:

> He was despised and rejected by men;
> > a man of sorrows, and acquainted with grief;
> and as one from whom men hide their faces
> > he was despised, and we esteemed him not. . . .
>
> He was oppressed, and he was afflicted,
> > yet he opened not his mouth;
> like a lamb that is led to the slaughter,
> > and like a sheep that before its shearers is silent,
> so he opened not his mouth. . . .
> And they made his grave with the wicked
> > and with a rich man in his death,
> although he had done no violence,
> > and there was no deceit in his mouth.
>
> *Yet it was the will of the* LORD *to crush him;*
> > *he has put him to grief* (Isaiah 53:3, 7, 9-10).

All four Gospels recount how Jesus was arrested, abandoned by his friends, falsely accused, mocked, spat upon, flogged, pierced with a belittling crown of thorns for claiming to be a king, then crucified. The noted German scholar Martin Hengel reminds us that "crucifixion was not just any kind of death. It was an utterly offensive affair, 'obscene' in the original sense of the word. . . . a punishment in which the caprice and sadism of the executioners were given full rein."[2] It was so torturous, in the slow and painful nature by which death finally came, that only the very worst criminals were subjected to it by Roman law.

The night before his crucifixion, Jesus knelt down and prayed,

> "Father, if you are willing, remove this cup from me. Nevertheless, not my will, but yours, be done." And there appeared to him an angel from heaven, strengthening him. And being in an agony he prayed more earnestly; and his sweat became like great drops of blood falling down to the ground (Luke 22:42-44).

Jesus was facing the cruelest death ever invented and was suffering it as the worst among wicked men. The weight of the pain and the shame is clear. After his arrest and torture, "they took Jesus, and he went out, bearing his own cross, to the place called the place of a skull, which in Aramaic is called Golgotha. There they crucified him" (John 19:16-18). This date in history has come to be called Good Friday.

Why is it called *Good* Friday? It is called Good Friday because, on the cross, God glorified himself by demonstrating his wrath against guilty sinners *and* by manifesting his love for them *at the same time.* It is called Good Friday because on the cross we see the justice of God maintained *and* the mercy of God obtained. It is called Good Friday because this is the work of God, *when grasped by faith,* that transforms our guilt over sin into a gladness toward God and causes us to live resolutely to the praise of his glory!

WHY DID CHRIST HAVE TO SUFFER THE CROSS?

Not only did the prophet Isaiah tell us what was to happen to God's promised Rescuer—how Jesus would suffer rejection, humiliation, and execution under the curse of God—he told us *why:*

> Surely he has borne *our griefs*
>   and carried *our sorrows;*
>   yet we esteemed him stricken,

smitten by God, and afflicted.
But he was wounded for *our transgressions;*
  he was crushed for *our iniquities;*
upon him was the chastisement that brought us peace,
  and with his stripes we are healed.
All we like sheep have gone astray;
  we have turned every one to his own way;
and the LORD has laid on him
  the iniquity of us all (Isaiah 53:4-6).

We can understand why powerful men, jealous of the power Jesus demonstrated and the acclamation he generated, might seek to have Jesus humiliated and executed as a criminal. What is harder to grasp is why God would purposely *send* his own beloved Son into the world and subject him to this humiliation and injustice. Isaiah's answer is, "He was wounded for our transgressions; he was crushed for our iniquities." Jesus took our punishment.

Sadly, many well-meaning but unreflective spiritual teachers have denied that the cross is about divine punishment at all. They do so because they believe that the idea of an angry God—and the idea that "every transgression or disobedience [must receive] a just retribution" (Hebrews 2:2)—is contrary to the love of God. For example, in their book *Forgiveness: A Guide for Prayer,* Jacqueline Syrup Bergan and S. Marie Schwan write,

> The death of Jesus is not, as has been commonly assumed by many, the result of an offended God punishing a "stand-in" for sinful humanity. We need to approach the Crucified, and see how much we are loved, to see there the kind of love that would prompt our own willingness to give our life for someone we love. And we can, even within the limitations of human loving, imagine ourselves dying for our spouse, children, friends. What seems impossible is to die for someone else, unknown, unloved. And what seems even more impossible, is that someone would do that for me. This is precisely what Paul says God has done for us in Jesus.[3]

I would agree that the apostle Paul says that, out of God's great love for us, Jesus died. But this death is not like the examples Bergan and Schwan give. If I see a Mack truck barreling down the street and about to hit my son Elliot, my love for him will compel me to run and push him out of the way, even if that means my getting hit and dying. Great love may even cause me to do this for a stranger. Still greater love may cause me to do this for the thug who just stole my wallet and darts away without looking. Men have dived off bridges to save a drowning man and died in the process. Soldiers have thrown themselves on grenades to save their buddies. These are all great acts of love. But these are *not* good comparisons to Christ on the cross, because they miss the essential point. The Mack truck, the deadly danger, in this case is God! The grenade that Jesus threw himself on for our sake is the death-inflicting explosion of his own wrath. If we look to Paul to grasp the meaning of the cross, then let us humbly consider *everything* he said: "God shows his *love* for us in that while we were still sinners, Christ died for us. Since, therefore, we have now been justified by his blood, much more shall we be saved by him from the *wrath of God*" (Romans 5:8-9). If this is not the case—if the danger we need to be saved from is not the wrath of God himself—then what *was* the danger Jesus rescued us from? If there is no danger, why not just *tell* us he loves us and zip back to heaven? Why did he need to *suffer* and *die* to complete his mission, if we are not in the crosshairs of future suffering and death?

The cross was not a heroic, impulsive act of self-sacrifice to shield us from an unfortunate accident or a dangerous situation. The cross was God's *intentional* and *punitive* action. "It was the *will of the* LORD to crush him; *he* has put him to grief" (Isaiah 53:10). Remember: the "him" in that verse refers to Jesus! Jesus was "smitten *by God*" (53:4). Bergan and Schwan may say, "The death of Jesus is not, as has been commonly assumed by many, the result of an offended God punishing a 'stand-in' for sinful humanity." But Isaiah says it is precisely that! "He was wounded for *our* transgressions; he was crushed for *our* iniquities" (53:5).

Lest there be any doubt that this suffering is punitive in nature, Isaiah says, "The *punishment* that brought us peace was upon him" (53:5, NIV).

It is precisely because it was substitutionary *punishment* that God declares the cross of Christ to be the highest demonstration of his *love* toward those who repent and put their hope in him. "In this is love, not that we have loved God but that he loved us and sent his Son to be the propitiation for our sins" (1 John 4:10). *Propitiation* is a rare word. At the heart of it is the idea that, in the person of his Son on the cross, God turns upon himself his just and irrevocable wrath against sin and sinners. "God shows his love for us in that while we were still sinners, Christ died for us" (Romans 5:8). On the cross, God vents his righteous wrath and displays his unfathomable love.

GRASPING THE TRUTH OF THE CROSS

The heart of the Christian message has been and always will be that "Christ died for our sins" (1 Corinthians 15:3). But in spite of this, many remain hamstrung by their secret guilt and are living very shallow lives. Why is that? I suspect it is because they have nothing but a shallow understanding of the cross, and in many cases only a small appetite for learning more. Eyes roll at the mere mention of the words *doctrine* and *theology*. These are verbal sleeping pills for many. Yet at the same time they suffer the insomnia of guilt, anxiety, and powerlessness in their faith. They lack confidence and purpose and wonder why. Could it be that a shallow understanding of the cross is like an inoculation shot? It prevents us from getting the real thing—a full-blown case of sin-uprooting, praise-inspiring, life-altering faith in Christ based on the radical implications of his death on the cross.

First Corinthians 14:20 urges us, "do not be children in your thinking. Be infants in evil, but in your thinking be mature." That is what we must do. We must think a little more. Only a truth-soaked *mind* can reshape our opinions, attitudes, responses, and decisions. This is the awesome implication of Jesus' words, "If you abide in my word, you are truly my disciples, and you will know the truth, and the truth will set you free" (John 8:31-32). Therefore it is vital that we keep tracking the outworking of God's grace on the cross.

In believing that Christ died for our sins, we are taking a firm grip on two life-liberating truths at work in the cross. The first is that

Christ died for *all* of our sins. First John 1:7 says, "If we walk in the light, as he is in the light, we have fellowship with one another, and the blood of Jesus his Son cleanses us from *all* sin." What good would it be if Christ paid the penalty for just half of my sins? What good would it be if he died for all but one of my sins, if that sin deserves an eternal punishment? When I put my hope in Christ, I am receiving by faith that Christ's substitutionary, self-sacrificing death covered over *all* my offenses, so that nothing remains to hinder God's pure love being poured out on me.

The second liberating truth that faith grips dearly is that Christ suffered the *full* punishment justly due for *each* of our sins. Each offense is appropriately and completely dealt with. We trust that "if we confess our sins, he is faithful and just to forgive us our sins and to cleanse us from all unrighteousness" (1 John 1:9). This means that anything that would leave a stain of guilt upon us, the smallest mark of unrighteousness, is punished and purged away through the atoning blood of Jesus.

Why is this so liberating for us who believe? Because it means that God is *right* to pardon and restore us to himself and would be *wrong* not to do so. I consider this a stunning truth. We, who became aware of our sinfulness and the justice of God's wrath against us, now have that same eternal commitment to justice working in our defense! "Shall not the Judge of all the earth do what is just?" (Genesis 18:25). If my sins are fully punished on the cross, and yet I am punished with hell, then my crimes have been punished twice! But the law of justice that demands that I be punished for my sins also *protects* me from being punished twice for the same sins. Justice will not allow it. All the righteous requirements of God's moral law regarding my sin have been carried out on the cross. This is the point made in Romans 8:3-4: "[God] condemned sin in the flesh, in order that the righteous requirement of the law might be fulfilled in us." "For our sake he made him to be sin who knew no sin, so that in him *we might become the righteousness of God*" (2 Corinthians 5:21). The result is that nothing sinful and unpunished now hinders the free flow of God's love toward those who put their faith in Christ. God can say, "I will love them *freely*, for my anger has turned from them" (Hosea 14:4). He is *justified* to show mercy, and with mercy to give us everything we need to live a life pleasing to him.

GOD'S REPLY TO A COLLECT CALL FROM PRISON

A few years ago I received a collect call from a prison. It was from a man I had met some weeks earlier in the projects, not more than four blocks from my house. This young man struck me as something of a scammer. He was brash and cocky, talking big plans but clearly without a bright future. I liked him immediately. I told him I was a pastor and later I even sent him a little note. Now he was calling me *collect* from the state penitentiary. He was serving a three-to-five-year sentence—for rape! He told me my note was the first personal letter he ever received in his whole life. He asked if I would write a letter for him to the judge. I countered with an offer to visit him instead.

It is sad to think of a child growing up so unloved as to never receive a birthday card or a valentine. This young man was fatherless, and his mother was an alcoholic. Sitting in that cell was a wounded young man. But he was also wayward. I did not want to be scammed. To rape a woman is an immeasurably wicked act of violence and an affront to a just and caring God. Rapists *deserve* jail. Justice demands it. I cared about this young man, but I needed to care also about the well-being of the women in my neighborhood.

If it were not for the cross, I would not have known what to say. But here is what I did try to communicate to him over a series of visits (later he was released and I lost track of him). I told him that God is a God of love, and therefore a God of mercy and forgiveness. But I told him first that God is a God of holiness, that he loves righteousness and is angry at him for the harm he had done. I assured him that God could show mercy to him, but not until he saw how wicked and evil his action was and how much he deserved to be punished.

I did not say, "Hey, God loves you, so let's just forget that you forced yourself on that young girl, and how much pain and terror you brought her." I said, in effect, "If you agree with your accuser and admit that you did evil and deserve to be punished by God, and if you turn to him who is rightly angry and ask him for mercy, then you will find that he is able to forgive you. How so? Because God calculated the full amount of punishment needed to vindicate the young woman's dignity, and he calculated the punishment needed to repair the glory of God defaced by your wickedness. Then he totaled it all up and inflicted the full punishment, in righteous anger, on Jesus Christ on the cross. And if you will entrust your life to the living Christ and obey him, trusting that the cross is sufficient payment for your sins, God will credit it as your own and will redeem your life."

GOD'S ANSWER TO THE PRAYER OF ELIE WIESEL

We can also hazard a guess now as to how God might answer Elie Wiesel's prayer. Remember, he prayed, "God, merciful God, do not have mercy on murderers of Jewish children." God's answer is the cross. I think he would say something like, "Elie, your passion for justice does you credit. I am committed to always acting justly and ensuring that justice is carried out. My love of justice will ensure that all sinners, from the least to the greatest, from you even down to the murderers of Jewish children, are punished. For the impenitent, 'the gloom of utter darkness has been reserved' [2 Peter 2:17]. For the penitent who put their hope in me, their full punishment has been meted out through the fiery wrath and terrible punishment that I poured out on my beloved Son.[4] Therefore, consider how great is my work on the cross of Christ, and put your trust in me."

The reason we can be sure that God's answer would follow this line is because Romans 3:25-26 affirms that the cross is a *demonstration* of God's commitment to uphold justice, ensuring that even his mercy toward those who trust him is justifiable. "This was to show God's righteousness, because in his divine forbearance he had passed over former sins. It was to show his righteousness at the present time, so that he might be just and the justifier of the one who has faith in Jesus."

Before the cross, God's forgiveness of even people like Abraham, Moses, and David *appeared to be unjust*. After all, they were pardoned and no punishment was meted out. Imagine what Uriah might have thought had he seen David joyously welcomed into the kingdom of

God. David had seduced his wife, betrayed him with a smile, and murdered him. Might he not have called God's justice into question? "Shall not the Judge of all the earth do what is just? Did you not declare, 'I will not acquit the guilty!' And isn't that just what you did?" If Uriah had made that case, he probably would have been told to wait and watch. God would justify his mercy toward David in due time.

When the time came, God sent Christ to the cross to justify the mercy he had shown David centuries earlier and to show that, indeed, David's sins, including those committed against Uriah, were fully punished. In the outworking of this unspeakable grace, David and Uriah were also reconciled. Uriah, grasping the truth of the cross, saw that God was vindicating him in righteous wrath. David, grasping the meaning of the cross, saw in Christ a substitute punishment for his wickedness. Both knew that God's justice was upheld, even as mercy broke through.

HOW CAN WE KNOW THAT SUCH GOOD NEWS IS TRUE?

Do you see now why the Christian message is called good news? But is it too good? How do we know it is true? We know because Acts 17:31 says God "has given assurance to all by raising [Jesus] from the dead." The resurrection of Jesus Christ is God's *validation* that all that Christ did in both his life and his death on our behalf was acceptable and pleasing to God.

The resurrection *validated* that Jesus was himself *sinless* and that he died for *our* sins, just as he said. Acts 2:24 says, "God raised [Jesus] up, loosing the pangs of death, because it was not possible for him to be held by it." Why did the justice of God make it impossible for Jesus to stay dead? It was impossible for Jesus to stay dead because he had lived a perfectly righteous life and therefore death, as God's just punishment for sin, had no crime against God to pin itself to. On the streets of Boston, the kids salute the law of justice by saying, "If you can't do the time, don't do the crime." In the case of Jesus, the voice of justice says, "He can't do the time, 'cause he did no crime."

The resurrection assures us that when Jesus claimed to be God's promised Rescuer and when he claimed to have the divine authority to forgive repentant sinners who put their trust in him, he spoke the truth. If he had been lying, he would not be sitting at the right hand of God but suffering the penalty due him for deceiving millions of people into trusting a false messiah. Instead, he was *"declared* to be the Son of God in power according to the Spirit of holiness *by his resurrection* from the dead" (Romans 1:4). The resurrection is God's stamp of approval on Jesus' claim to be our Lord and Savior.

The resurrection also sharply defines what it must mean to have faith in Christ. *Because* Christ has been raised from the dead, we are not putting our faith in merely a historical event but in a living, death-conquering, and reigning Savior. Our faith is *based* on something in the past, but it is *placed* in One who is very much alive today. Notice how the apostle Paul speaks of faith in terms of a living Christ: "I have been crucified with Christ. It is no longer I who live, but Christ who *lives* in me. And the life I now live in the flesh I live by faith in the Son of God, who loved me and gave himself for me" (Galatians 2:20). Paul is living by faith in the living Christ. And he prays that this would be our normative Christian experience: "that according to the riches of his glory he may grant you to be strengthened with power through his Spirit in your inner being, so that Christ may dwell in your hearts through faith" (Ephesians 3:16-17).

HOW DO WE LIVE BY FAITH?

What kind of faith so connects us to Christ that he is able to live in our hearts? How do I live by this faith? Colossians 1:22-23 teaches us how to grasp the truth of the cross *by faith:* "he has now reconciled [you] in his body of flesh by his death, in order to present you holy and blameless and above reproach before him, if indeed you continue in the *faith, stable and steadfast, not shifting from the hope of the gospel that you heard."* The kind of faith that connects us to Christ is dependent, persevering, and hope-filled.

Saving faith requires a sense of dependence on the strength, wisdom, and integrity of another. I have "saving faith" when I yield to the ambulance crew following an accident. In the present case we are depending on Christ. Another word for this is *trust*. I trust you when

I am entrusting something to you and depending on you for it. To believe in somebody means the same thing. Biblically, these words (*faith, trust, belief*) are interchangeable. The word most broadly misunderstood is the word *believe*. In surveys that ask, "Do you believe in God?" the answer is nearly always "Yes." People say, "I believe," meaning they accept certain doctrinal or religious ideas to be true. This is not saving faith, however, because nothing is at risk, nothing is entrusted, nothing hangs in the balance. Even demons are said to believe in God in the noncommittal sense of acknowledging his existence or attributes (see James 2:19). They would gladly like to believe that "Jesus died for my sins," if that were all that faith required.

Saving faith puts all the eggs in one basket. It never believes in Christ as well as other religious systems. It does not believe in the sense of saying, "I had better cover my bases." It says, "I will stake my soul on Christ and the cross. I will live for this one thing: Christ and him crucified." To believe is to commit, to entrust, and to pursue the life of Christ.

Saving faith also has a persevering quality to it.[5] I may put my faith in God at some decisive and memorable moment, but inherent in the act is a commitment to be faithful *all my life*. I must persevere in my commitment before I can fully say I was faithful. I did the same thing in my marriage. At a decisive moment, June 10, 1978, at 4:30 in the afternoon, I gave my life to my wife. But what I gave her in faith was a promise to love her faithfully. The true meaning of the word *faithfully* becomes evident by the fact that I can substitute it for the words *all my days*. "I promise to love you, Kristen, all my days!" The word *faithfulness* makes no sense if persevering, lifelong trust is not inherent in it. That is why Paul says you are reconciled "if you *continue* in your faith . . . *not moved* from the hope held out in the gospel" (Colossians 1:23, NIV).

WHY DOES GOD WANT EVERYTHING TO FLOW THROUGH FAITH?

The reason God wants all his benefits to flow to us through our faith in Christ is because the alternative method would be to have us earn them as we earn a paycheck. Why does God consider this bad? After all, if we want a nice car, do we not have to work hard to pay for it? If I want a beautiful house, do I not have to pay for it? If things are given to me, do I not in fact value them less than if I earned them by the sweat of my brow?

Nevertheless, God's forgiveness does not come as an earned income credit. "For by grace you have been saved through faith. And this is not your own doing; it is the gift of God, not a result of works, so that no one may boast" (Ephesians 2:8-9).

Why does God's grace come by faith alone? To ensure that it is seen by all as the gift of God! A paycheck can never be a present. In order to protect the gift-like quality of his grace, God commands us to receive it *freely*, through faith alone. After all, there is a lot more joy in giving a gift than in meeting a payroll, and God *delights* in being a giver of good gifts.

When my son Nathanael turned fifteen, we bought him a new, adult-sized bike. This kind of gift is highly unusual for us, so I was excited about the surprise it would be for him. My satisfaction as the gift giver was the joy of seeing his face light up. He was delighted to receive it, and I was delighted to give it. The same is true with our redemption.

I would not have felt more honored if Nathanael had said, "Gee, Pop, this is great, and I promise you I will not ride it until I have taken the garbage out for a month without being asked." I would have been pleased to see him do that, for sure, but not as a *payment* for the bike. I would have been disappointed if he had felt he needed to pay for my gift. Then it would no longer have been a gift! I would have been saddened as well, because, given the rate at which teens forget things, he probably would never have been able to ride his bike. It would also have said something about our relationship that I would not have liked. I am his father, not his employer. My joy is in his "Wow!" So it is with God and his gift. His reward as a gift giver is in the gladness of heart that we experience in receiving his gift *as a gift*.

Another reason we cannot pay for our sins by doing various good works as a tradeoff for God's mercy is so that no one can boast: "For by grace you have been saved through faith. And this is not your own doing; it is the gift of God, not a result of works, *so that no one may boast"* (Ephesians 2:8-9). Anything we do with a motive of adding to the work of Christ so as to win the forgiveness of God becomes the ground of self-satisfaction in our own goodness, rather than trust in God's grace. If my son earns a bike, he has himself to be proud of. Every bike previous to this one he did earn and purchase on his own. This was good, and I was proud of him. In giving him this bike, I wanted to communicate something different, something of my joy in him as my son. He lost all boasting privileges, other than the boast of having a father who loves him and knows how to give good gifts. Among the forgiven there is no boasting either, no sense of having earned anything—only the unending praise for so great a gift, secured at so great a cost and given so freely by the God of all love.

THE SOUL ON ITS KNEES

A saying often attributed to Victor Hugo is that, "There are moments when, whatever the posture of the body, the soul is on its knees." Standing before the cross of Christ is one of those moments. Archimedes, with his lever in hand, boasted, "Give me where to stand and I will move the earth."[6] But Jesus Christ, with his shoulder to the cross, moved something immeasurably harder. He moved heaven's judgment from its course and directed it to himself, absorbing it all until every evil in us that justified the wrath of God was fully punished. He did this so that his Father's blazing love could freely, abundantly, and righteously flow toward those who put their faith in Jesus Christ.

THE HUMAN EXPERIENCE OF GOD'S OUTWORKING GRACE

In the outworking of God's grace, God sent his Son to die on the cross to justify his complete forgiveness of repentant sinners based on the complete punishment Jesus suffered in their place on the cross. The human experience of this Great Work lies in grasping the truth of the cross and entrusting our lives to the living Christ, whom God raised from the dead, that we might be assured that in Christ, we have been reconciled to God.

GROUP STUDY QUESTIONS

1. Elie Wiesel's prayer points to the fundamental problem of how a just and holy God can forgive sinners and still be just and holy. How does the cross of Jesus Christ answer this problem?

2. How does the cross fulfill the promise made to Abraham on Mount Moriah?

3. According to Isaiah 53, *why* did Christ have to suffer and die to fulfill God's promise?

4. What connects us personally to the benefits of the cross? Regarding our sin, what two things does our faith believe were accomplished on the cross on our behalf?

5. What does it mean to be "justified by faith"? Why is God just to be merciful to repentant sinners? How does this turn our hope in God into a strong assurance of God's loving-kindness?

6. What does the resurrection of Jesus affirm, according to the Bible? How did the realization that Christ is alive and reigning define for the apostle Paul what it meant to trust in Christ? What does he mean when he says, "I have been crucified with Christ" (Galatians 2:20)? According to Romans 6, how do we experience our own death and resurrection?

7. What are the attributes of genuine saving faith according to our anchor text, Colossians 1:21-23? How has your faith shown itself as *perseverance*?

7

THE GREAT WORK EXPERIENCED

Fighting for a Clean Conscience

A peace above all earthly dignities, a still and quiet conscience.
—WILLIAM SHAKESPEARE, *HENRY VIII*

Let us draw near with a true heart in full assurance of faith, with our hearts sprinkled clean from an evil conscience and our bodies washed with pure water.
—HEBREWS 10:22

The washing away of shame and guilt[1] is properly the *experience* of God's Great Work that accompanies our faith in Christ. When Nana and three of her friends came to see me, our conversation reminded me how awesome and immediate the cleansing power of the gospel is when gripped by faith.

Nana was a young mother I and others had helped get through some very difficult times through our local pregnancy help center. On this day Nana brought her friends in to see the beautiful Lennart Nilsson pictures made famous in *Life* magazine. They reveal the beauty of a baby growing in the womb. As the women passed the pictures around excitedly, one of them turned to me. A solitary tear dripped down her cheek and she said, "I had an abortion two years ago. It hurts so bad in my heart. Is there anything I can do?"

Before I could answer, another of Nana's friends said, "You can fast. Fasting will help a lot." Nana agreed quickly that fasting might help relieve her friend's guilt. In their way of thinking, past wrong behavior is counterbalanced with good behavior or self-punishing behavior. In this case they were hoping that fasting would pay down on the debt of guilt their friend felt and cause her to feel better.

Synthesizing a longer conversation than here represented, I smiled and said, "Fasting is a good thing but not in this situation. I doubt, first of all, given how tenderhearted you are, that even if you fasted to the brink of starvation, you would feel any sense of assurance that you had paid *in full* for the guilt you feel in your heart. But I want you to know that God is pleased with your tears and your confession. What you did was wrong. God is angry when we kill his children. But because God wanted to show you his great love, he sent Jesus Christ into the world to suffer the full punishment due all your sins. Christ did this by dying on the cross, after which God raised him up again. You honor him best, not by fasting, but by trusting in Christ for the forgiveness of your sins. This means believing that the terrible suffering Christ endured on your behalf is sufficient even for the sin of child-killing."

Nana's friend looked up, and another tear fell from her eye. "That is the most beautiful story I have ever heard," she replied. It was the word *beautiful* in her response that indicated to me that she had heard the gospel in her heart. It showed me again that believing is cleansing!

EXPERIENCING FORGIVENESS

The punishment that Christ bore on our behalf—a complete punishment for all our sins and a just punishment for each of them—cleared the way for the free flow of God's mercy. In terms of our human experience, putting our faith in Christ and his Great Work on the cross means that we *experience* this mercy as a clean conscience and a bold, expectant confidence in drawing near to God. That too is part of the Great Work. The cross and our trust in the cross are akin to a gate being opened and a gate being entered.

Returning to our anchor text we read, "And you, who were once alienated and hostile in mind, doing evil deeds, he has now reconciled in his body of flesh by his death, *in order to present you holy and blameless and above reproach before him . . .*" (Colossians 1:21-22). Christ is our righteousness. He makes us blameless and above reproach. Agreeing with this means having our consciences satisfied in the work of the cross in the same way that God is satisfied—*completely.* Hebrews 9:14 stresses this very point, applying the work of the cross to our burdened conscience: "How much more will the blood of Christ, who through the eternal Spirit offered himself without blemish to God, *purify our conscience* from dead works to serve the living God." The blood of Christ is a cleansing blood. It washes away wrath *and* it removes the stain of self-condemnation.

CHRIST BORE OUR SHAME

Christ died to remove our *shame* as well as God's anger. By shame I mean simply the emotional pain we feel over past sinful behavior. Shame can be imposed on us, too. We can be *put to shame* when our sin is known by others. Their contempt can cause us shame. All of this Christ bore on the cross. He was *humiliated* in the events leading up to the cross. He suffered humiliation on the cross. He "endured the cross, despising the *shame*" (Hebrews 12:2). Therefore, "whoever believes in him will *not* be put to *shame*" (Romans 9:33).

CHRIST EARNED US PEACE OF MIND

Still another way the Bible expresses the human experience of God's forgiveness is to speak of our *peace* with God. Romans 5:1-2 says, "Since we have been justified by faith, we have *peace with God* through our Lord Jesus Christ. Through him we have also obtained access by faith into this grace in which we stand, and we rejoice in hope of the glory of God." Though we were once enemies, God has made his peace with us through Christ. His peace with us has been ratified by blood and signed by our repentance and faith. We enjoy this peace as *peace of mind.* We are at peace with God. We shall sleep in peace (Proverbs 3:24). We will awake knowing his mercy is ours and is new every morning. On this we must stand.

CHRIST MAKES US CONFIDENT TO PRAY

Through Christ "we have also obtained *access* by faith into this grace in which we stand" (Romans 5:2). "In [Christ] we have boldness and access with *confidence* through our faith in him" (Ephesians 3:12). "If our heart does not condemn us, we have *confidence* before God; and whatever we ask we receive from him . . ." (1 John 3:21-22). The benefits of believing are a clean conscience and a radical confidence to approach God as a child approaches a father (Matthew 7:7-11), that is, expectantly. We can praise him and petition him and seek his guidance and ask for his favor because we are reconciled. The way is open. We are now called children of God and can run to him as a heavenly Father, expecting good things from him (Matthew 7:7-11). "Let us then with *confidence* draw near to the throne of grace, that we may receive mercy and find grace to help in time of need" (Hebrews 4:16).

INSTRUCTING OUR CONSCIENCE ABOUT THE CROSS

Not that this sense of liberty is always there and never flags. It surely does. One problem is that our conscience is not sufficiently informed about the gospel. It needs training in righteousness. In terms of human experience, we must often "reassure our heart before him; for whenever our heart condemns us, God is greater than our heart" (1 John 3:19-20). I take this to mean that we need to bring the work of God in Christ to bear on our stubborn conscience. We must grasp the truth of the cross and wrestle our conscience into alignment and conformity. We must instruct our conscience about the cross until our conviction of guilt gives way to joy and confidence. Hebrews 10:22 calls this having "our hearts sprinkled clean from an evil [burdened] conscience."

When my conscience condemns and blocks the way to God, I must be ready to stand on the truth of the gospel and contend for my faith.

By faith, I look to the heavens and shout, "Oh happy day!"

Conscience shouts back, "I object."

I reply, "On what basis?"

Conscience says, "You did such-and-such. How can you possibly think God does not see it?"

I admit, "I will not deny the facts, and God knows the tears that have been shed over it. But I ask, 'Was it or was it not a sin for which Christ died?'"

Conscience demurs, "Well, yes."

My faith takes the offensive, "If yes, was it or was it not paid in full?"

Conscience pauses, "I withdraw the objection."

Faith presses further, "And should you not also *rejoice* with me?"

Conscience is awestruck by the all-sufficiency of the cross. And faith says, then let us draw near to God and say, "Thank You, Father, for paying for that awful sin my conscience has just brought to mind. I rejoice all the more deeply in your loving-kindness."

We can truly say, "There is therefore now no condemnation for those who are in Christ Jesus" (Romans 8:1). Such is the cleansing power of the cross, when grasped by faith, on a stained conscience.

FIGHTING FOR A CLEAN CONSCIENCE

Some things, such as dandelions, never seem to go away for good. Shame and guilt can be like that. They constantly reassert themselves and keep us from experiencing the joy of a "good conscience toward God" (1 Peter 3:21, NIV). What makes persistent shame a serious problem is that it belies a persistent *unbelief* in the sufficiency of Christ to atone for our guilt. It calls the truth of the gospel into question. And that is a serious matter.

DISCONNECT THE DOTS

One way that shame calls the gospel into question is by constantly interpreting life's hardships as a sign of God's continuing anger for our past evil behavior. Persistent shame whispers, "God is punishing me." An amazing example of this is found in Genesis 42. Joseph's brothers, in a fit of jealousy and resentment over God's blessing on Joseph's life, sold him into slavery. They lied to their father, telling him Joseph was mauled by a wild animal. They kept this wickedness a secret for decades!

Yet, when things went wrong (and don't they always!), the voice of persistent shame hurled condemnation upon them. At one point, Israel was experiencing a famine and the brothers went to buy food from the Egyptians. If you know the story, you know that at this time the Egyptian administrator of grain distribution was Joseph himself. The brothers negotiated with him for food without any idea whom they were talking to. When things went bad in the negotiations, one of the brothers interpreted their trouble, saying, "In truth we are guilty concerning our brother, in that we saw the distress of his soul, when he begged us and we did not listen. That is *why* this distress has come upon us" (Genesis 42:21). This is *decades* after the event! But shame is persistent. Things committed forty or fifty years ago can still persistently gnaw away at us.

One reason for this is obvious. Like the brothers of Joseph, perhaps we have never come clean. We have never repented. We merely lop off our guilt feelings like we mow down dandelions. As soon as we do not see it, we think it is not there. After a season, the thing pops up again and we lop it off again. In this mode, we will never get relief because we are really back at the starting point of admitting our guilt.

However, sometimes the problem is due to an oversensitive conscience and a serious fault in our understanding of God—in other words, weak theology! A friend who suffered a house fire confided to me once, "I think God is punishing me for not doing the things I should be doing as a Christian." I was so grieved to hear this. God does *discipline* those he loves, but he *punishes* those he loves not by burning their house down but by sending his Son into the world to suffer our due punishment on the cross. My friend's comment reflected a serious defect in her faith. She will never experience the full assurance of God's loving-kindness if she thinks God burned her house down for poor devotional habits. God is grieved that we should think him so quick-tempered and irrational.

Yet, because sin has warped our thinking about who God is, it is natural for us to play connect-the-dots when things go wrong. One day when my oldest son, Nathanael, was only six and still new at riding a bike, he fell off and scraped his knee. Earlier that day I had disciplined him for some minor offense and had already forgotten about it. Nathanael had not forgotten. As I wiped away his tears and tended to his bleeding knee, he looked up and said, "I think God let me fall off my bike because of what I did this morning."

I said, "No, Son, he did not. He let you fall off your bike so that you would learn to overcome hardships and develop a persevering character.[2] When God wants to send a message that you have done something wrong, he does not send you a bike accident, he sends your mom and me to tell you directly and clearly. You do not have to guess. When he wanted to *punish* you for your sins, he sent his own Son to die on the cross as your substitute punishment. Understand?"

That may sound like a lot of theology for a lad of six, but in fact it made good sense to him. He was relieved. He loved me for saying it. He got up on his bike and tried again.

If God is punishing us through the hardships of life, then the cross cannot be our complete atonement,[3] and the apostle Paul overstated the case when he said, "There is therefore now no condemnation for those who are in Christ Jesus." Some lingering judgment must be causing bad things to happen. But the truth is, "since we have been justified by faith, we have peace with God through our Lord Jesus Christ" (Romans 5:1). Daniel Fuller draws out the idea by translating Romans 5:1 this way: "Since we have the forgiveness of sins and God is no longer our enemy but our Father, we can allow his peace to rule in our hearts, *despite life's sufferings.*"[4]

FORGET ABOUT FORGIVING YOURSELF

A second way persistent shame expresses itself is in the words "I know God forgives me; I just cannot forgive myself." This is evidence of a shallow understanding of the cross. I realize that when we first begin to grasp the enormity of our guilt, and before we have had a chance to grasp the extent of Christ's sufferings, we are likely to be angry with ourselves and think that we ought not forgive ourselves even if God does. This would be the voice of immature faith, not unbelief. It is the spiritual equivalent of living through that awful Saturday between

Good Friday and Easter morning: one truth is clear, but the full truth is still a day away. Even so, any attempt to live the Christian life in the Saturday mode is doomed to fail. Christ is risen!

Current and prevailing ideas on forgiveness have much to say about forgiving yourself. Sadly, there is more in these books on forgiving yourself than on how it is that God forgives. God is mentioned; but restoring our self-esteem is the focus. Usually a number of steps are given to help people forgive themselves. I am not persuaded that this is a sufficient method for defeating persistent shame. I see no evidence of it producing radical joy and muscular faith. It is quite possible that God is insulted by it. I know this may sound harsh, if not shocking, but bear with me. If we admit that God forgives us but we do not forgive ourselves, are we not insulting his judgment and exalting our own, as if we have a higher standard of justice than he does?

The reason we do not see this at first is because humility is a Christian virtue, and to say, "I know that God forgives me but I cannot forgive myself" sounds humble. But beneath the surface we are apt to find a fiercely proud sense of having better judgment than God.[5] The very question of *self*-forgiveness may reflect a resistance to glory in God's mercy and a preference to grind our teeth for failing to be as good as our pride always assured us that we were.

One way to silence this voice of self-condemnation is to humbly remind ourselves that the Christian experience of forgiveness makes us God-centered, not self-centered. So the Christian way of thinking is to say, "If God is satisfied, who cares what others think? Even my own judgment ought not to matter. If God has assured me of his mercy, I will exult in his mercy and rest in his judgment." This is precisely how Romans 8:31, 33-35 teaches us to reason ourselves forward:

> If God is for us, who can be against us? . . . Who shall bring any charge against God's elect? It is God who justifies. Who is to condemn? Christ Jesus is the one who died—more than that, who was raised—who is at the right hand of God, who indeed is interceding for us. Who shall separate us from the love of Christ?

Here is our standing point. Here is the Christian's confidence.

THE ONLY UNFORGIVABLE SIN

When we allow ourselves to shift our concern from God's judgment to our own, not only do we exalt our judgment above God's but we also belittle the entire work of Christ. In effect we are saying, "It is not good enough." It is at this precise point that the most severe warnings in the Bible come. We are questioning the sufficiency and effectiveness of the Great Work itself. Jesus said sternly,

> "Every sin and blasphemy will be forgiven people, but the blasphemy against the Spirit will not be forgiven. And whoever speaks a word against the Son of Man will be forgiven, but whoever speaks against the Holy Spirit will not be forgiven, either in this age or in the age to come" (Matthew 12:31-32).

Admittedly, this is a difficult verse to grasp. What does it mean to "speak against the Holy Spirit"? Taking our cue from the rest of Scripture, we can observe that the entire work of God's forgiveness and reconciliation, the Great Work, is attributed to the *outworking power* of God, the Holy Spirit. Hebrews 9:14 says it was *"through the eternal Spirit* [that Christ] offered himself without blemish to God." First Peter 3:18 says Christ was "made alive *in the spirit."* Our belief in the truth and our commitment to trust in Christ is called the "sanctification of the *Spirit"* (1 Peter 1:2; 2 Thessalonians 2:13). Therefore, the one thing God will not tolerate—indeed, the only thing he ultimately refuses to forgive—is the sin of discounting the Great Work of grace wrought by the Spirit of God. This is the unforgivable sin, for it belittles the central work of the cross and calls it insufficient or unnecessary.

Once we have discovered how much Christ suffered in love to justify his mercy toward us, and once we have learned that he rose from the dead to be our living Lord, if we then conclude, "Not good enough," we are *unbelievers.* Since *persistent* shame is a form of *persistent* unbelief in the sufficiency of the cross, this warning applies as well:

> If we go on sinning deliberately after receiving the knowledge of the truth, there no longer remains a sacrifice for sins, but a fearful expec-

tation of judgment, and a fury of fire that will consume the adversaries. Anyone who has set aside the law of Moses dies without mercy on the evidence of two or three witnesses. How much worse punishment, do you think, will be deserved by the one who has spurned the Son of God, and has profaned the blood of the covenant by which he was sanctified, and has *outraged the Spirit of grace?* . . . Therefore do not throw away your confidence (Hebrews 10:26-29, 35).

To "outrage the Spirit of grace" echoes the earlier warning against "blasphemy against the Spirit." The point is that if we are to be afraid of anything, or ashamed of anything, it should not be the evil behavior in our past but rather our *present unbelief*—that we could look at the suffering of Christ and think it not good enough to cleanse us from *all* unrighteousness and reconcile us to God. Remember this when battling against guilt feelings arising from particularly selfish, gross, or violent sins. Christ agrees that our sin is damnable, but because of his great love for us he suffered the *full* penalty due for all and each of our damnable acts. We must meet persistent shame with persistent faith in the sufficiency of Christ for our salvation.

THE MEDICINAL VALUE OF SHAME

Does this mean I should never feel ashamed? It is good to make a distinction between things that happened long ago that have been set right, as far as is possible, and things that we do in the ongoing struggle against sin that we have persistently refused to admit responsibility for. In the first, we honor God by accepting the cleansing of our consciences. In the latter, we honor God by being ashamed of ourselves and turning from our present sins by the grace of God.

Even though King David was assured of forgiveness, he still wrote Psalm 51 expressing shame and sorrow over his sin. He confessed to doing "evil in [God's] sight" (51:4). I am happily married, but that does not mean I am never sad or angry with myself for saying or doing things that hurt my wife. My ability to sorrow or feel ashamed is one reason I can maintain a long-term, happy relationship with her, and she with me.

When our problem is not persistent, unwarranted shame over

things long forgiven but rather a persistent, sinful habit not yet faced, shame has a medicinal value. It is a necessary inducement to true repentance. Paul used it on one occasion, regarding an obstinate brother. He recommended, "Have nothing to do with him, *that he may be ashamed. Do not regard him as an enemy, but warn him as a brother"* (2 Thessalonians 3:14-15).

Until I permit myself the *short-term* painful experience of shame or self-loathing, until I hate what demeans God's glory and hurts others, my heart will never be converted and I will never have the strength to change.

CRACKED BUT NOT BROKEN

In contrast, "the unjust knows no shame" (Zephaniah 3:5). I once befriended a man who worked a steady job, had some wonderful kids, had a godly wife, and was in church every Sunday. He was also a crack addict. He repented and wept repeatedly over this. But what was always lacking in his tears, and always made his repentance false and ineffective, was a true and deep godly sorrow and sense of shame for all the lying and stealing and abuse involved in his addiction. He was sorry when he got caught. He was not ashamed. He was embarrassed before his wife and sons, but he was not alarmed, indignant, ready to wage war against an enemy out to kill him and his family. He was not sick of his sin. He was only sick of the consequences. He needed the medicine of shame. Unfortunately, none of the many rehab programs he tried subscribe to the notion of shame. They think the problem is low self-esteem and that it would be shameful to tell a person to be ashamed of himself. But there is such a thing as a healthy shame that leads to a healthy zeal to overcome a habitual sin.[6] A healthy fear of God produces a healthy hatred for sin.

TENDING THE GARDEN OF CONSCIENCE

Shakespeare called a still and quiet conscience "a peace above all earthly dignities." A peaceful conscience makes for bold prayers, passionate praise, confident service, courageous suffering for the sake of righteousness. It makes for healthier long-term relationships and sound sleeping. But when we lose our peace—and we all do—then we must be prepared to humble ourselves before our gracious God. The loss of peace signals the need for self-inspection and action. In striving to live by a clear conscience, we must learn to do a little weeding and watering. I have found the following to be basic in tending to the garden of our conscience.

Allow a season of sorrow for sin. When I feel bad for being bad, I feel good. It means my conscience is working. It means God's Spirit is at work in me. It is painful and shameful, but it is godly sorrow and it leads to repentance.

Rest in the truth of the gospel. A good conscience weeps for a short time, then comes to rest again in the gift of God in Jesus Christ. Where else am I to go but back to the cross? In this way shame spurs change but does not become persistent or disabling or demeaning to the work of Christ. We must trust Christ as both "the founder and *perfecter* of our faith" (Hebrews 12:2).

Restore what is restorable. Part of what it means to repent is to restore what is restorable. Sin, after all, does provide fleeting pleasures. In renouncing it, it is important that we not continue to benefit from it. Therefore restoration is part of repentance (see Luke 19:1-10). For example, if I have embezzled, repentance, faith, and my desire for a clean conscience will compel me to return the money. It may also ask me to pay a fine to ensure that the pain of sin consciously outweighs the pleasure of sin. If I am afraid of the consequences, I will still return the money; it is just that now I will learn the discipline of daily prayer. I will learn how much Christ can be trusted with my life. Making restitution where possible cleanses the conscience. It goes a long way in restoring relationships, too.

Remember that God forgets. In striving for a good conscience, there is a place to let things go. In Jeremiah 31:34, the Lord instituted a covenant with his people: "For I will forgive their iniquity, and I will *remember* their sin no more." The word *remember* is not used in a cognitive sense. God is omniscient, after all. It is used in a relational sense. He will not hold our sins up to us as a barrier to our ongoing fellowship with him. In this sense he renders them forgotten. He removes our sin and shame and deposits them into the deepest part of the sea. "There," as Corrie ten Boom once said in her wise and child-like way, "He posts a sign, 'No fishing allowed.'"[7] In striving for a good conscience we need to remember to forget.

Endure hardship as God's discipline, not damnation. As God's children, we experience the ongoing work of God's conviction but there is no condemnation. Here is one of the places that the truth must be used as a shield and wielded as a sword. Hebrews 12:7, 10-11 reminds us of the distinction:

> It is for discipline that you have to endure. God is treating you as sons. For what son is there whom his father does not discipline? . . . For they disciplined us for a short time as it seemed best to them, but he disciplines us for our good, that we may share his holiness. For the moment all discipline seems painful rather than pleasant, but later it yields the peaceful fruit of righteousness to those who have been trained by it.

Bear scars graciously. It is no small lesson that the risen Lord, utterly transformed in his glorified body, still maintained his nail scars. Our scars remain as a testimony to the outworking *grace* of God. Scars offer a reminder of a wound. They also testify to having been *healed.* We may choose to hide the scars of our past sin in shame and guilt, or bear them graciously as a testimony to the grace of God. The ongoing consequences of some of our sins are not reminders of our sin, they are reminders of the Great Work on our behalf. In this way, our triumph over shame is completed. What guilt and shame once used to blackmail us into silence, God now uses to make our testimony ring authentic and glad of heart. "Let me tell you about the Great Work of God in my life . . ."

THE HUMAN EXPERIENCE OF GOD'S OUTWORKING GRACE

The washing away of shame and guilt is properly the experience of God's Great Work that accompanies our faith in Christ.
We cleanse our conscience by relishing the sufficiency of Christ and the cross and running like children to our Heavenly Father.

GROUP STUDY QUESTIONS

1. Many of us struggle with persistent shame and guilt over past behavior. How do we know that God wants to set us free from this burden? In what ways does the Bible teach us that Christ died to cleanse our consciences?

2. Romans 8 instructs us how to fight for a clean conscience and defend against feelings of condemnation and shame. What truths do we need to stand on in wrestling with guilt and shame? Can you share an example of your own battle with shame and guilt?

3. Why is persistent shame a true threat to Christian faith? How does persistent shame negatively affect us and those we love?

4. What might you say to someone who says, "I know God forgives me, but I cannot forgive myself"?

5. What is the true and only unforgivable sin? How do we turn from it?

6. When is shame medicinal and proper rather than destructive and belittling to the sufficiency of Christ's death for sin?

7. We have considered the idea of "tending to the garden of conscience." Discuss the ways we do that and give an example of doing that or needing to do it.

8

THE GREAT WORK ENJOYED

Living Under the Influence of Grace

My sin—O the bliss of this glorious thought—
My sin, not in part, but the whole,
Is nailed to the cross, and I bear it no more:
Praise the Lord, Praise the Lord, O my soul!
—HORATIO G. SPAFFORD,
"IT IS WELL WITH MY SOUL"

Sing aloud, O daughter of Zion;
  shout, O Israel!
Rejoice and exult with all your heart,
  O daughter of Jerusalem!
The LORD has taken away the judgments against you.
—ZEPHANIAH 3:14-15

Fred lay in a hospital bed, so pickled from years of alcoholism that he was near death. The day he drove to the detox center, he had a coffee mug full of Scotch with him and sat in the parking lot gulping it down before checking in. Meanwhile, without his knowledge, his wife, Diane, prepared to file divorce papers. She had watched him slide into drunkenness and had suffered his abusive language and lying for far too long. The man she once loved, she now hated. He had destroyed their marriage and left the family in disarray.

Fred lay in his bed with alcoholic hepatitis, liver damage, and bronchial pneumonia. He had lost bowel control, the lining of his stomach was shot, and he was jaundiced. The hospital contacted Diane and warned her to prepare for his death. Fred lay on his bed, shaking with tremors and weeping with remorse. "I felt so ashamed, like such a failure and so alone," he later told me. After many days of remorse and confession, he caught a glimpse of God's loving-kindness. He had tasted it before. Some twenty years earlier God had wooed him to faith. He had responded initially; but like so many, he had failed to live under the daily influence of grace, and therefore his faith was ineffective. Now, lying in his bed, he felt the grace of God wooing him once again. He resolved to put his hope entirely in the hands of God and never to drink again. He remembers saying, "If I live, I will serve the Lord."

Diane was confused and uncertain. She turned to a relative, who counseled her to put her hope in God. Believing that God might have something better in mind, she tore up the divorce papers. She made sure Fred got the medical attention he needed. She told Fred of her secret plans to leave him, her decision to stay, and why. The Sunday following Fred's dismissal they were together in church. She prayed for Fred's healing. Fred prayed for God to give him the resolve to repair their marriage as far as was possible, and he asked his wife for forgiveness.

Their small local church was soon riveted by their unfolding story. Here was a couple headed for divorce—if death did not get there first. Now they were alive and together before the throne of mercy! Fred never drank again. Over the subsequent years, I watched Fred change under the ongoing, outworking influence of God's grace, until his final breath, when Fred succumbed to cancer.

Fred's story is awesome, but it is not unusual. It follows the biblically revealed course for the normative Christian experience of God's Great Work. Initially, God's grace spared Fred's life; subsequently, it changed his life. Initially, he experienced God's grace in the forgiveness of his sins; subsequently, he experienced it as a conquering power over sinful habits. Initially, grace saved his marriage; subsequently, it repaired his life as a man, a husband, a father, a laborer, a neighbor, and a citizen.

OUR JOY AND GOD'S GLORY

Fred was *glad* to be forgiven, *thankful* to be sober, and *happy* to learn God's will for his life. He *enjoyed* his new relationship with God, his family, and his local church and was pleased to serve where needed. His wife was overjoyed. Many people saw with their own eyes the work of grace and marveled at it. All of this bubbled up as praise to God. Jesus said that all heaven breaks out in radical rejoicing over the Great Work of God's grace:

> "What man of you, having a hundred sheep, if he has lost one of them, does not leave the ninety-nine in the open country, and go after the one that is lost, until he finds it? And when he has found it, he lays it on his shoulders, rejoicing. And when he comes home, he calls together his friends and his neighbors, saying to them, 'Rejoice with me, for I have found my sheep that was lost.' Just so, I tell you, there will be more joy in heaven over one sinner who repents than over ninety-nine righteous persons who need no repentance" (Luke 15:4-7).

If the angels of heaven rejoice so freely when one sinner, such as Fred, repents, imagine the immeasurable joy of heaven in the ongoing work of grace among multitudes. "Let the heavens be glad, and let the earth rejoice" (Psalm 96:11). In the outworking of God's grace, we rejoice and God is praised:

> Sing to the LORD, bless *his* name;
> tell of *his* salvation from day to day.
> Declare *his* glory among the nations,
> *his* marvelous works among all the peoples!
> For *great* is the LORD, and *greatly to be praised* (Psalm 96:2-4).

Of this, John Piper explains,

God's quest to be glorified and our quest to be satisfied reach their goal in this one experience: our delight in God overflows in praise. For God, praise is the sweet echo of his own excellence in the hearts of his people. For us, praise is the summit of satisfaction that comes from living in fellowship with God.[1]

A HEART GLAD TO WORSHIP GOD

Once the lyrics of the gospel have been written on our hearts, the melody of the gospel bursts forth as a song of gladness and praise to God: "Rejoice and exult with all your heart, O daughter of Jerusalem! The LORD has taken away the judgments against you" (Zephaniah 3:14-15). Our everlasting peace with God is also our everlasting joy in God. Notice the linkage in Romans 5:1-2: "Therefore, since we have been justified by faith, we have *peace* with God through our Lord Jesus Christ. Through him we have also obtained access by faith into this grace in which we stand, and we *rejoice* in hope of the glory of God." Where *peace with God* is established, *pleasure in God* erupts.

We are like Munchkins in Oz. When the house fell on the wicked witch, they called to one and all, "Let the joyous news be spread, the wicked old witch at last is dead!" So in our case the fatal blow against our enmity with God has been given. His just anger is fully vented; the just penalty is fully paid; the righteous requirements of the law are fully met in Christ. Our guilt and shame are fully purged, the desire for sin is mortally wounded, God's love is unrestrained, and the Spirit of Christ is dwelling in us as a down payment of heaven itself. An open invitation to petition him has been granted. The hope of glory has been given. "Let us rejoice and exult and give him the glory" (Revelation 19:7). "For you, O LORD, have *made* me glad by your work; at the works of your hands I *sing* for joy" (Psalm 92:4).

Hymns, songs, prose, poetry, paintings, stained glass windows, steeples pour endlessly out of Christian faith in humble attempts to put into words or forms our inexpressible joy in the Great Work of God on our behalf.[2] I have prayed a thousand times the rich words of Edward Taylor:

Lord, feed mine eyes then with thy doings rare,
  And fat my heart with these ripe fruits thou bear'st
Adorn my life well with thy works; make fair
  My person with apparel thou prepar'st.
  My boughs shall loaded be with fruits that spring
  Up from thy works, while to thy praise I sing.[3]

A HEART GLAD TO OBEY GOD

Those whom God *declares* righteous, he *makes* righteous: "You shall be clean from all your uncleannesses . . . and I will give you a new heart, and a new spirit I will put within you. And I will remove the heart of stone from your flesh and give you a heart of flesh. *And I will put my Spirit within you, and cause you to walk in my statutes and be careful to obey my rules*" (Ezekiel 36:25-27). The New Testament word for this is sanctification (2 Thessalonians 2:13). It refers to the ongoing work of God's Spirit to make us holy, as he is holy. This work is not completed in a day. We do not plant lettuce in the morning and expect a salad for supper. The growth of righteousness imitates natural growth. It takes time to show itself, just as the lettuce seed takes time to look like lettuce. But Christians desire to grow up into a reflection of Christ, to the honor of Christ, or they are not Christians. The grace that pardons *always* purifies.

Why can I say this so absolutely? Because Titus 2:11-12 says the grace of God that brings salvation always produces Christlikeness: "For the grace of God has appeared, bringing salvation for all people, *training* us to renounce ungodliness and worldly passions, and to live self-controlled, upright, and godly lives in the present age." The grace that brings *salvation* goes on to train us to live a godly life. A sanctified life is not optional to salvation; it is standard equipment. Other things may be called grace, but they are not *saving* grace.

The human experience of this sanctifying work is desire. It is a *glad* obedience. We pray, "I *desire* to do your will, O my God; your law is within my heart" (Psalm 40:8). "We make it our *aim* to please him" (2 Corinthians 5:9).

Does this mean that we *never* feel resistant to God or never want things our way or never feel a desire to please our flesh? It is probably most people's experience that we feel embarrassing amounts of resistance and that our obedience is a halting, sputtering devotion. By a glad obedience I mean that the *desire for holiness* is planted in our hearts through faith in Christ, and we are obtaining it by faith over time. "No one born of God makes a practice of sinning, for God's seed abides in him, and he cannot keep on sinning because he has been born of God" (1 John 3:9). This seed is God's gift of holiness. It asserts itself against our naturally disobedient and self-centered tendencies so that we wrestle against the evil behavior we used to relish. God's grace lays siege against those sins fortified by habitual practice. Conviction strikes and intensifies. A healthy fear of God and a growing love of God bang away at the habit. The Word of God teaches us the value of repentance and prayer and brotherly accountability, all of which are part of God's continuing grace to free us from habitual sins.

We find an analogy to the steady force of God's grace in the autumn leaves. What makes them cling so tightly throughout the summer, in spite of all the storms that blow through, and then let go on a still autumn day and fall like colored snowflakes? The answer is that underneath the base of the stem, a new bud is forming, pushing, nudging, and eventually unhinging the old leaf. We do not see the evidence of this until six months later when it swells and bursts forth as a new leaf, but it is there nonetheless. In the same way, God has put into our heart a new life principle. It is a love for righteousness, and as it grows it nudges old habits till they drop. Over many years we can see this governing principle in the changed life it produces. Or, we will not see it, and thus will rightly call into question the reality of our repentance and question whether we really are under the grace of God.[4]

Does this mean that Christians never sin at all? What about those times when I feel cold toward God and I lose the desire to please him? Do I lose my standing with God? Sin always costs us something. We are deceived if we think it does not. But I think the best way to get at the answer is to illustrate rather than analyze.

SHEEP STUMBLE, BUT SWINE WALLOW

Sheep and swine can both end up in the mire. Yet the essential difference in their two natures is quite visible from the reaction each has to its fallen condition. While sheep do stray and stumble into the mire, they quickly loathe the situation and struggle to get free. They may be dirty, but they desire to be clean. They may be stuck, but they bleat for their shepherd to come and save them out of the muck. But swine, in keeping with their nature, wallow in the muck, content to stay there all day.

When professing Christians behave badly, we are confused by the inconsistency. No matter what one's theology might say about assurance of salvation, where unbelief, disobedience, and sinful habits persist, there is an ever-shrinking inner witness of belonging to Christ. Those observing this persistent lack of an obedient heart in a professing Christian will also lose confidence about the authenticity of that profession. A person who *consistently* says one thing while acting out another is called a liar. "Whoever says 'I know him' but does not keep his commandments is a liar, and the truth is not in him" (1 John 2:4).

But authentic Christians can and do fall under temptation and into the mire of sin. Their actions are often inconsistent with the way of righteousness. It is more a sign of immaturity or weakness, not hypocrisy. The apostle Paul prepares us for this: "Brothers, if anyone is caught in any transgression, you who are spiritual should restore him in a spirit of gentleness" (Galatians 6:1).

Contrast this with 1 John 3:6: "No one who abides in [Christ] keeps on sinning." One passage forewarns us that a brother will be "caught in a sin," the other that true brothers do not continue sinning as before. How do we reconcile these two? I believe the answer goes back to understanding our nature. Do we have a sheep nature or a pig nature? If we have a pig nature, like a pig we will not only fall into the mire but will scramble for it; we will hunker down into it and roll our backs in it. We will live in sin, defend our sin, and surround ourselves with others in sin.

As we have already observed, every authentic Christian is given a new nature by the regenerating power of God's Spirit (Ezekiel 36:26-27; 1 Peter 1:3). It is part of the Great Work. It is the nature of a sheep before a shepherd. We may fall into the mire because we temporarily refuse to follow the shepherd. But once in the mire, we desire to get out and we bleat for help. We willingly receive the restoration offered by mature Christians who come to advise us on how to overcome our sin through godly sorrow, accountability to others, and growing deeper in the grace of God. This is one way we are "proved genuine" (1 Peter 1:7, NIV) and "make [our] calling and election sure" (2 Peter 1:10). Sheep stumble, but swine wallow. What we *are* may be difficult to discern when we are covered in mud. But our reaction to it, over a period of time, will tell us if we are a part of God's flock or the Devil's herd.

A HEART GLAD TO LOVE GOD

Living under the influence of God's grace means not only a new and growing passion for his glory, not only a new and growing desire to be like him, but a new and growing love for him. Peter Kreeft said, "Christianity is not a hypothesis, it is a proposal for marriage."[5] When God says, "I will be their God, and they shall be my people" (Jeremiah 31:33) he is saying something very similar to, "I will be your husband, and you will be my bride." It is covenantal language. We find it again in Isaiah 62:4, 5:

> You shall no more be termed Forsaken,
>   and your land shall no more be termed Desolate,
> but you shall be called My Delight Is in Her,
>   and your land Married;
> for the LORD delights in you,
>   and your land shall be married. . . .
> And as the bridegroom rejoices over the bride,
>   so shall your God rejoice over you.

These are marriage vows of sorts. God's delight in his people caused him to plan and pursue us as a man pursues the love of his life.

I remember how I plotted and arranged to marry my wife, Kristen. There were talking points to be broached ever so delicately. Feelings had to be confirmed and solidified. There were fears to allay and expectations to be understood. There was a formal proposal to be made, and that had its own planning and preparation to it—all very enjoyable. There was shopping to be done—for not just any diamond ring but the right one. "How can I find out what she likes?" "How can I earn the money to buy it?" More planning and plotting.

Then schedules needed to be considered, and arrangements for our life together after the wedding needed to be thought through. With ring in hand, further plots had to be hatched, surprises had to be set up. All of this joy was in just the anticipation of our union. Then there was the joy of making the actual proposal. At the solemn moment I breathed deeply and asked Kristen to marry me. With joy I slid the ring on her finger. This joy kept building as the wedding was planned over the following months. The rehearsal heightened the joy because it signaled the nearness of the consummation. Then there was the ceremony itself, waiting formally for her to walk the long aisle in all her radiance, where we pledged to live together faithfully, as long as we both shall live. Then of course there was the intimate and intense joy of consummated love as two become one flesh. Twenty-seven years later, love continues its joyful work, laboring to sustain our union through life's pressures, disappointments, and curve balls.

God's work in pursuing us is a *labor of love,* marked by this same joy, only purer and deeper. "As the bridegroom rejoices over the bride, *so shall your God rejoice over you"* (Isaiah 62:5). He enjoys the wooing of our heart's affection away from sin and self and to himself. As his bride, we are united with him in the bond of Eternal Love. We are won over to love the Lord our God with all our heart, mind, soul, and strength (Luke 10:27).

HARDSHIP IS NO LASTING IMPEDIMENT TO A HEART GLAD TOWARD GOD

There are times when events and circumstances make us feel as if God has rejected us. On these occasions our tears are our food day and night (see Psalm 42:3). We wonder if God has turned his back on us or forgotten us. We can feel such numbing pain and loss at certain times that living seems a terrible burden. We openly wonder how we can go on. How do we reconcile this reality with the unshakable gladness of heart that is ours in the grace of God?

In this life, tears and joy are incompatible only if we fail to remember that our joy is *in God* and is not tethered to any circumstances in this temporal life:

I will greatly rejoice *in the* LORD;
    my soul shall exult *in my* God,
for he has clothed me with the garments of salvation;
    he has covered me with the robe of righteousness (Isaiah 61:10).

Jesus agonized on the cross for the joy of something beyond the cross (see Hebrews 12:2). So with us, our emotions are linked to our present circumstances and life experiences, but peace and joy are deeper than emotions. Emotions rise and fall as we experience on a rotating basis poverty and plenty, good health and sickness, a few good breaks and then a string of "bad luck." Into every person's life story are written unexpected tragedy and suffering and the certainty of sickness and death. This present life offers only fleeting pleasures and seasons of good times. The gladness of heart we are talking about is deeper and higher than this world. It is nothing less than an abiding, trusting confidence in God's goodness in spite of present experiences; and it's not uncommon for the deepest peace and our most unspeakable joy in God to come in the midst of tremendous personal trauma. We experience joy not as sunshine but as a ballast keeping our ship afloat throughout the raging storms of life.

WHEN SORROWS LIKE SEA BILLOWS ROLL

Horatio Spafford (1828–1888) was a prosperous lawyer in Chicago in the years following the Civil War. He invested his money in shoreline property on Lake Michigan and was able to give generously to the work of Christian ministry, using his buildings to help reach the urban poor and to contribute to the global ministries of his personal friends, the famous evangelist D. L. Moody and the well-known hymn writer Philip Bliss. Spafford had a wife and five children—four daughters and a son. Then a series of tragedies hit Spafford that would have broken the faith of anyone not anchored in the true grace of the gospel.

First, their young son died of pneumonia. As Spafford and his wife struggled in their grief, their friends urged them to take a vacation to England and join Moody in his campaigns there. Spafford resisted because he was at that time renovating some buildings in

Chicago to help the YMCA outreach. Then in 1871, just four months after the death of their son, the Great Chicago Fire hit, burning two thousand acres of property, including all of Spafford's. His friends again urged him to get away and rest. Little could be done about the loss. He arranged passage to London for his family and himself, except that two days before departure he was forced to appear before officials who were trying to sort out ownership claims after the fire. Spafford sent his family ahead and planned to follow on the next boat.

A few days into the crossing, the ship collided with another in a fog bank. It sank in twelve minutes. The initial reports were very hopeful; there were many survivors. Then Spafford received a telegram from his wife: "Come quickly, I alone survive. Your beloved wife."

All four of his young daughters were gone. As he steamed for London, he asked the captain to notify him when the ship reached the point where his daughters had gone down. There he wept and poured out his heart to God. As he watched the sea billows roll, he thought of God, his sovereignty, his mercy, and all his promises. Then he wrote down his thoughts and, later, his friend Philip Bliss put them to music. The result has become one of the church's greatest hymns of praise, "It Is Well with My Soul":

When peace like a river attendeth my way,
When sorrows like sea billows roll—
Whatever my lot, Thou has taught me to say,
It is well, it is well, with my soul.

Though Satan should buffet, though trials should come,
Let this blest assurance control,
That Christ has regarded my helpless estate
And hath shed His own blood for my soul.

My sin—O the bliss of this glorious thought—
My sin, not in part but the whole,
Is nailed to the cross, and I bear it no more:
Praise the Lord, praise the Lord, O my soul!

And Lord, haste the day when my faith shall be sight,
The clouds be rolled back as a scroll:
The trump shall resound, and the Lord shall descend,
"Even so"—it is well with my soul.

Spafford's gladness makes room for much weeping. But it will not be overcome. Our gladness is in God, and ultimately, in God alone. This gladness is inaccessible to the darkest powers of this corrupt world. No one can take away our joy unless he can figure a way to take God away from our hearts. In the history of God's saving grace, no example of this has yet been found. Tragedy cannot. Persecution cannot. Poverty cannot. As Paul says in Romans:

> Who shall separate us from the love of Christ? Shall tribulation, or distress, or persecution, or famine, or nakedness, or danger, or sword? . . . No, in all these things we are more than conquerors through him who loved us. For I am sure that neither death nor life, nor angels nor rulers, nor things present nor things to come, nor powers, nor height nor depth, nor anything else in all creation, will be able to separate us from the love of God in Christ Jesus our Lord (Romans 8:35, 37-39).

THE GLORY OF THE ORDINARY

In contrast to Spafford's extraordinary experience, I think it best to close with the ordinary. God's promise of an outworking grace is for all his people, "from the least of them to the greatest" (Jeremiah 31:34). Most of us have rather mundane life experiences, but we undergo the same influence of God's grace. And there is glory here too.

Gene is the most ordinary man I know. He is average in height and appearance, in intelligence and skills. He loves pizza and sports. Nothing about Gene is going to grab your attention. Yet Gene is a heroic figure to me because, by his quiet and God-honoring life, he has demonstrated the power of living under the influence of God's grace.

Gene's memories of his youth are painful and stir up bitterness inside him. He is reluctant to speak of it. By the time he reached his twenties he was drinking and drugging himself into oblivion. Several times he was homeless, and as he says, "properly so." One day Gene woke up from a drunken stupor to realize that he had drunk a can of beer that had been used as an ashtray. Gene knew he was in trouble. He sought temporary help numerous times. Once he was sober for a whole year, then took one drink and within a week was getting plastered every night. He was alienated from his family, from society, from himself, from God. Then Gene gave his life to Christ.

What happened as a result? Did he become a great leader, write a great hymn, start a famous ministry, or lobby for great social justice? No, he simply filled his life with God and threw away his bottles. For several years he worked steadily as a taxi driver and then started painting houses. He went to church every Sunday, attended various Bible studies, and began to serve the people wherever he saw a need.

A few years later he fell in love with a woman in my church and for three years he gently and persistently pursued her. I took them through premarital counseling and conducted their wedding. In the meantime, Gene went to school for computer-assisted design (CAD). Soon he had a full-time job in design. No more taxi driving for Gene. After two years of marriage they bought their first house. When Gene was forty, he and his wife had their first baby.

Gene has given time on Wednesday nights to working with the homeless in Boston. He gives monthly support to a variety of ministries. He knows his neighbors. All this change happened slowly but steadily over a fifteen-year period.

First Thessalonians 4:11-12 says, "Aspire to live quietly, and to mind your own affairs, and to work with your hands, as we instructed you, so that you may live properly before outsiders and be dependent on no one." This is Gene's testimony. It is a good testimony and full of glory in its own way. Most of us are average and ordinary. Yet we too will greatly glorify God's mercy in our lives if, as Gene did, we learn to live under the ongoing influence of God's grace. In one matter after another, let us look to God with a thankful heart, follow his ways, and "love our Lord Jesus Christ with love incorruptible" (Ephesians 6:24).

THE HUMAN EXPERIENCE OF GOD'S OUTWORKING GRACE

God's Great Work includes his sanctifying grace, where he slowly yet persistently changes our speech, our personal habits, our demeanor, our priorities in life, and our decisions. He teaches us how to live, how to love, and how to serve. The human experience of this outworking grace is a glad heart in learning to live under the influence of God's Holy Spirit.

GROUP STUDY QUESTIONS

1. In this chapter I said, "Where *peace with God* is established, *pleasure in God* erupts." How has your pleasure in God and your praise for God grown as you have grasped the Great Work? What Scriptures have most assisted you in the glad worship of God? What song or poem expresses your pleasure in God?

2. The Bible also includes the book of Lamentations as well as psalms of brokenness, tears, and grief. How do these fit into our worship of God? According to James 4:1-10, when is it more appropriate to weep than to rejoice?

3. According to Ezekiel 36:25-26 and Jeremiah 31:31-34, what does God's true grace accomplish over time in those whom God forgives? How does this differ from what some people are seeking when they ask for God's grace? In what ways has the outworking power of God's grace begun to work itself out in your own life?

4. What is meant by the idea that, "Sheep stumble, but swine wallow"? How is obedience a sign of true faith in God? What are we to make of professing Christians who are persistently disobedient? Would you assure them, or warn them?

5. How is it that marriage is a useful metaphor for describing the outworking grace of God? Do you feel there is a "marriage" being lived out between you and God? In what ways do you "work" at this marriage?

6. What has been the greatest disappointment, pain, or hardship in your life that has threatened your love for God or your willingness to trust him? How does Spafford's hymn, "It Is Well with My Soul," testify to the lasting and inseparable power of God's love in Jesus Christ?

9

THE GREAT WORK SHARED

Pushing Past Our Grudges

Of him that hopes to be forgiven, it is indispensably required that he forgive. On this great duty eternity is to be suspended.
—SAMUEL JOHNSON, *THE RAMBLER*

If you do not forgive others their trespasses, neither will your Father forgive your trespasses.
—MATTHEW 6:15

As a student at Bethel College, in Minnesota, I remember the school president, Dr. Carl Lundquist, saying, "You never really find out what is inside a man until he is bumped and you see what spills out." He was illustrating the link between forgiveness received and forgiveness extended—a link so strong that the one confirms the presence of the other. God in his providence ensures that we all get plenty of chances to show what is inside us. We will suffer these bumps either with increasing bitterness or as our finest moments when the grace of God unmistakably and radiantly spills forth. Therefore, learning to push past grudges is crucial to growing winsome and healthy as a Christian and finally obtaining the full measure of grace that brings eternal life.[1]

THE NECESSITY OF FORGIVING THOSE WHO HURT YOU

If we have experienced God's grace, we are under a moral imperative to extend it to others. It is part of "the obedience of faith" (Romans 1:5). This means we obey God, not in order to win his favor and earn his mercy, but out of our growing confidence in him as our God. Daniel Fuller's illustration is worth remembering. He says that when I *obey* my doctor's orders I am expressing *faith* in my doctor. If I do not, my doctor will say, "Find a doctor you *trust,*" meaning one you'll *obey*.[2] One of the clearest orders given by the Great Physician of our souls is that we *must* forgive those we hold grudges against: "Forgive your brother from your heart" (Matthew 18:35).

I'M ON THE HOOK AND I CAN'T GET OFF

From the earliest days, those who received grace and mercy from the Lord were compelled to extend it toward those who hurt them. God delivered Israel from bondage and established a relationship based on faith, saying, "I will walk among you and will be your God, and you shall be my people" (Leviticus 26:12). As their sovereign Lord, God commanded them,

> "You shall not hate your brother in your heart, but you shall reason frankly with your neighbor, lest you incur sin because of him. You shall not take vengeance or bear a grudge against the sons of your own people, but you shall love your neighbor as yourself: I am the LORD" (Leviticus 19:17-18).

Notice that the command to forgive does not mean denying the reality of someone's evil or rationalizing the wrong into a justifiable right (that is what the wrongdoer does). There is a place to call sin *sinful* and wrongdoing *wrong*. Silence can be a form of passive agreement with what is going on. "Reason *frankly* with your neighbor, lest you incur sin because of him." But that done, God calls us to stay clear of hatred, thoughts of revenge, and the harboring of grudges. What is more, he commands us to love the unlovely people in our lives! The basis of this command is our faith in God as the watchman of our soul's health and happiness. "I am the LORD."

In the same way, the Lord Jesus also called us to push past our grudges. He forbade revenge or even spiteful thoughts. He echoed his own "Old Testament" voice, calling us to reject the common advice of every age and deal graciously with our neighbors. "You have heard that it was said, 'You shall love your neighbor and hate your enemy.' But I say to you, Love your enemies and pray for those who persecute you, so that you may be sons of your Father who is in heaven. For he makes his sun rise on the evil and on the good, and sends rain on the just and on the unjust" (Matthew 5:43-45). What kind of people can love like this? God's people do. When they are cut, they bleed grace; and in the process, they receive a transfusion of grace!

Anyone can live out the puny ethical creed "You scratch my back and I'll scratch yours." The children of God have a higher calling. "If you love those who love you, what benefit is that to you? For even sinners love those who love them" (Luke 6:32). When we return love for hatred, and prayer for a curse, eyebrows are raised. People see that God is *at work* in us because God's *outworking* grace is spilling forth from us.

STANDIN' IN THE NEED OF PRAYER

It is hard to forgive. It is unnatural. It is an altogether greater thing than merely saying, "I forgive you." Truly it is a Great Work to forgive from the heart. To bleed grace when cut will require a transfusion of grace. It is interesting that Jesus speaks of forgiving others in the context of prayer. Prayer is faith articulating its glad dependence on God's provision. In what is commonly called the "Our Father" or the Lord's Prayer, Jesus points us to the source of all grace and shows us the means by which we push past our grudges. Our means for doing this is prayer. Here our strong desire to be forgiven is linked to our weak desire to forgive others. We are to pray,

> "Our Father in heaven,
>   hallowed be your name . . .

forgive us our debts,
> as we also have forgiven our debtors . . ." (Matthew 6:9, 12).

Then the hook appears again:

> "For if you forgive others their trespasses, your heavenly Father will also forgive you, but if you do not forgive others their trespasses, neither will your Father forgive your trespasses" (6:14-15).

I have witnessed the extraordinary power of these words, and it has left me numb with the weight of its glory. I only knew Stephen for the last two years of his life. He was an Irish cussing cowboy wannabe. Born and raised on the streets of Boston, he moved to Texas and lived there for many years. There he ran guns, drank heavily, and fought with anybody he could bait by his small size—a dangerous lifestyle for a hemophiliac. In the mid-eighties he contracted the AIDS virus through tainted blood. Back in Boston, his brother, Tom, an elder in my church, prayed and waited.

One day Stephen learned that the boyfriend of a baby-sitter hired to watch his infant daughter had become annoyed by the baby's crying, beat the child, and threw her out in the backyard, where she was bitten by fire ants. She died a horrible death, and her killer was arrested and sent to prison. It was the hardest blow of Stephen's life, and he returned to Boston a broken yet seething man. In spite of many invitations, he refused to come to church. Every time I went over to the house, he scurried upstairs and out of sight.

A few months later his brother, Tom, got arrested for participating in a nonviolent sit-in at an abortion clinic. Tom went there to weep and repent for his own actions that had led to three abortions during his youth. This struck a chord in Stephen. In the pain over the murder of his own child, Stephen wanted to protest the killing of innocent children and so attended and got arrested at a subsequent sit-in in West Hartford, Connecticut.

Along with about three hundred other men and women, he was held in a state prison for almost a week before being released. Every day the men gathered for prayer, and Stephen heard many testimonies and listened quietly as the men prayed for themselves, their families, and for the end of the violence of abortion. About midweek, while in a circle of praying men, Stephen started to weep. He prayed, "God, I pray that you would *forgive* the man who murdered my daughter . . . forgive him . . . and please forgive me, too, for all I've done."

Stephen wanted peace with God. But he realized that to have it, he must forgive his enemy. He prayed just as Christ taught us all to pray: "Forgive us our sins, as we forgive those who have sinned against us."

Stephen came out of that prison radically changed. The Great Work worked quickly. Within a few months, it was not unusual to find Stephen helping the weak and visiting the sick in our community. He joked and laughed wildly with other Christian men. He came alive, even while he was dying. He visited Texas to set some things right with his ex-wife, then returned to Boston to live out his last days. In forgiving the man he hated most in this world, this hemophiliac got a transfusion of grace that healed him in ways that mere blood could never do. His last months were spent in a hospice, mostly with homosexuals dying of AIDS. While he could, he shuffled around visiting each one, telling a joke, cursing the sickness, telling them how he had received God's mercy, and praying with them. He died in great pain and in great peace.

We block the flow of mercy in our lives when we grip tightly to our grudges. Stephen came to see that his own ability to receive mercy was dependent on letting go of his grudges—no matter how justified they seemed. A wise Puritan once said, "He that demands mercy and shows none, ruins the bridge over which he himself is to pass."[3]

GETTING TOUGH ON THE CRIME OF UNFORGIVENESS

Jesus was betrayed by a disciple, falsely accused by those he came to serve, denied justice in the courts, abandoned by his friends, humiliated, beaten, and hammered to the cross and mocked till his dying breath. "When he was reviled, he did not revile in return; when he suffered, he did not threaten, but continued entrusting himself to him who judges justly" (1 Peter 2:23). His pain was fuel for prayer: "Father, forgive them, for they know not what they do" (Luke 23:34). We, too, must pray like this for those who have hurt us. And we must keep on praying. Persistent grudges must be met with persevering prayer until we obtain the grace to forgive.

In spite of Jesus' example and the testimony of people such as Stephen, we still think our case exceptional. "It's easy for you to talk about forgiveness," a man trying to be reconciled to a family member once told me. "You don't understand how badly he hurt me." He wanted sympathy, not surgery. He wanted understanding, not prescriptions. But he was on the hook. I did not put him there. I replied that forgiveness only counts when it hurts. We are not called to forgive the holy and the righteous. He was not pleased. He squirmed, but the hook did not bend.

I have enough of my own raw experiences to realize that this is pain talking. Grudges love to be nursed, not nuked. Given enough time and fertilizer, our grudges will grow so big they will wrap themselves around our very personality and cover us like ivy covers a house. Grudges force us to play the role of victims, never victors. Holding on to grudges is like crying out for a life preserver while clinging to the anchor! We have to choose either one or the other. "If you do not forgive others their trespasses, neither will your Father forgive your trespasses" (Matthew 6:15). Our grip on grudges must be released. Our very life depends on it.

IT IS THE RIGHT THING TO DO

Why can God be so unequivocal about conditioning our forgiveness on our willingness to forgive others?[4] Jesus answers this question with a parable. He tells of a king who was owed millions of dollars by one of his subjects. When the man could not pay his debt, the king ordered him, his wife, and his children to prison. The man begged for time. He promised to pay back everything. The king showed mercy. He pardoned the entire debt and let him go free. What follows in the story demonstrates the wickedness of someone wanting to receive mercy yet withholding mercy:

"When that same servant went out, he found one of his fellow servants who owed him a hundred denarii, and seizing him, he began to choke him, saying, 'Pay what you owe.' So his fellow servant fell down and pleaded with him, 'Have patience with me, and I will pay you.' He refused and went and put him in prison until he should pay the debt" (Matthew 18:28-30).

Here is an example of a man who acts in faith, all right—bad faith. When the king hears about it, he summons the servant and denounces him. He orders him to prison to pay all his debts. Then Jesus says, "So also my heavenly Father will do to every one of you, if you do not forgive your brother from your heart" (18:35). God will not tolerate his mercy being treated with contempt.

That is why I say forgiving others is crucial to finally obtaining the full measure of grace that brings eternal life. Initially, when someone asks humbly, confesses their need, and praises God for his forgiveness, we naturally will assume and hope that genuine saving faith has begun. But time confirms or denies the saving nature of our initial plea for mercy. If it proves to be bad faith by the bad reflection it casts in our behavior toward others, then it will be treated as such. If our faith produces a gracious spirit toward others, it will be rewarded with everlasting grace.

SAND IN THE EYE

Most of the wounds we bear come from people—often loved ones—whose selfishness and immaturity lead them to say and do insensitive things. Most of it flows from their own quiet rebellion against God. They inflict real hurts, but usually they are not consciously out to destroy us. In pushing past grudges, I find it helpful to distinguish between those hurts that come from being offended and those that come from being violated. One is more of an irritant, the other more of an injury. Of course, we can turn all our irritants into injuries.

On occasion the wind will gust and a speck of grit or sand will blow into our eye, slip in under the lid, and at once irritate us terribly. Our first urge is to rub our eye furiously. We hold back because we know that rubbing the sand in our eye only makes a bad situation worse. If rubbed, the whole eye will be inflamed and, perhaps, permanently damaged.

Similar urges and possible damage result when others irritate us by what they say or how they act, especially when they do it over and over and over again. We can slough it off once, maybe twice, and think ourselves gracious, but by the third time we are looking for a two-by-four and contemplating how many whacks it will take to correct the problem. They have gotten under our skin and irritated our very souls. Brooding over the behavior of others is like rubbing the sand in our eye. It does not take long before that relationship is raw and supersensitive. But the truth is, it was only a speck. It was a small irritant. It need not have caused us any real or lasting harm.

Peter asked Jesus about these sand-in-the-eye-folks: "'Lord, how often will my brother sin against me, and I forgive him? As many as seven times?' Jesus said to him, 'I do not say to you seven times, but seventy times seven'" (Matthew 18:21-22). We never get off the hook. We are not allowed to count. We are not allowed to say, "That's the last straw!" If it is the last straw, we are counting! What are we to do then?

Paul, who at the time was unjustly suffering *imprisonment,* wrote, "I therefore, a prisoner for the Lord, urge you to walk in a manner worthy of the calling to which you have been called, with all humility and gentleness, with patience, bearing with one another in love" (Ephesians 4:1-2). We are to love. Forgiveness is God's love *at work* in us, expressing its desire to push past grudges. Love shows itself as mercy, as loving-kindness, as patience, as forbearance. Love, in these various forms of self-expression, is like tears in the eyes; it washes away the sting of harsh words, thoughtless words, ill-timed words. Love purges out slights, a false witness against us, a betrayed confidence, an ill temper, and hundreds of other irritations of the heart.

Gary Thomas, a commentator for *World* magazine, said, "Mature Christians have a double standard. They are hard on themselves when it comes to sin, but gracious and gentle toward others."[5] That is right. Most of the strained relationships we have are due to sand in the eye that is rubbed raw. We have tried changing the person, attacking the person, giving the person the cold shoulder, or running from the person. But once again, the hook gets hold of us. The Great Work is working. Now we will try "bearing with one another and, if one has a complaint against another, forgiving each other; as the Lord has forgiven you, so you also must forgive. And above all these put on love, which binds everything together in perfect harmony" (Colossians 3:13-14).

IF A DOG CAN DO IT, SO CAN I!

I saw a vivid picture of this once when visiting a family who had a large German shepherd and a small child. While we were talking, the toddler toddled in and jumped on the big dog while it lay quietly on the floor. This dog, which can be a fierce watchdog, and certainly checked me out when I came to the door, was startled and disturbed. He felt the blow. But he looked up, saw who it was, and laid his head back down. I sat there amazed, watching the youngster roll around on the dog, pull its hair, playfully push and shove and make a nuisance of himself to the dog. The dog endured it all. He never snapped or growled, in spite of getting stepped on and yanked about fairly well. The dog's behavior said, "It's just that immature little tyke. He's no threat, just an annoyance. I can take it." God's grace, as an outworking power, has the capacity to love like that, bearing with the immature, the annoying, and the inconsiderate.

FALLING PREY TO THE WICKED

And then there are the wicked to consider. We are no longer talking about sand in the eye but fangs in the flesh. Psalm 52 identifies the nature of wicked man:

> Why do you boast of evil, O mighty man?
> The steadfast love of God endures all the day.
> Your tongue *plots destruction,*
> like a sharp razor, you worker of deceit.
> You *love evil* more than good,
> and lying more than speaking what is right (Psalm 52:1-3).

The wicked plot destruction. They grow strong by destroying others. Such people deceive, seduce, exploit, inflict pain—and love it.

Their consciences are seared (1 Timothy 4:2). They brutalize and betray others and laugh about it. They see every relationship as a win-lose competition. Everyone is to be conquered, and anyone who gets the best of them is the target of revenge. They wear suits and smile as often as they hang on the corners and dress like thugs. They are rich and poor, male and female.

Make no mistake about whether some people are truly wicked. When a mother sticks her child's hand in boiling water for childish behavior, that is wicked, and the wound goes far deeper than the burned flesh. That happened in my city. I ached with the young woman in our counseling center who told me that when she was fourteen, her mother's boyfriend came to her one afternoon and raped her. When she told her mother about it that night, *she* was kicked out of her own house, not the boyfriend. Her mother considered her daughter competition.

In business, in government, in families, there is no shortage of cruelty. History is a catalog of human wickedness, rising and falling and rising again. Its victims are random, just people in the way of where the wicked want to go. David fell prey to a wicked man by the name of Doeg. At the time David was a target of King Saul's jealousy and had to flee for his life. Though David was innocent of all wrongdoing (1 Samuel 20:1), he was forced to live in caves and find food as best he could to survive. He went to the house of Ahimelech, a faithful priest in the city of Nob, who gave him food. "Now a certain man of the servants of Saul was there that day, detained before the LORD. His name was Doeg the Edomite" (21:7). Later on, Doeg reported to Saul what the priest had done for David: "[Ahimelech] inquired of the LORD for him and gave him provisions" (22:10). Doeg knew that his report endangered the priest, but he wanted to ingratiate himself with Saul.

Ahimelech and his entire family were summoned. The other priests in Nob who failed to report the incident were also summoned and accused of treason. Saul ordered them *all* killed. Saul's soldiers refused to kill the priests because they were innocent and "priests of the LORD" (22:17). So Saul said to Doeg, "You turn and strike the priests" (22:18). Doeg did, and "he killed on that day eighty-five persons who wore the linen ephod. And Nob, the city of the priests, he put to the sword; both man and woman, child and infant" (22:18-19). Doeg slaughtered the entire village to win the favor of Saul. David broke when he learned of it. He felt responsible for it. He wrote Psalm 52 out of the anguish of soul inflicted by the wicked. Yet David plotted no revenge. He made room for the judgment of the Lord to deal with his Doeg, as we must ours:

> But God will break you down forever;
> > he will snatch and tear you from your tent;
> > he will uproot you from the land of the living (Psalm 52:5).

It is not wrong to draw comfort from the vindicating righteousness of God. God reassures us that he sees the wicked things men do and will avenge the pain they cause. "Beloved, never avenge yourselves, but leave it to *the wrath of God,* for it is written, 'Vengeance is mine, I will repay, says the Lord'" (Romans 12:19). The promise of God's vindicating wrath frees us from the entangling impulse of acting as a judge and executioner. We may leave it to God and comfort ourselves with Psalm 37:5-9:

> Commit your way to the LORD;
> > trust in him, and he will act.
> He will bring forth your righteousness as the light,
> > and your justice as the noonday.
> Be still before the LORD and wait patiently for him;
> > *fret not yourself over the one who prospers in his way,*
> > *over the man who carries out evil devices!*
> Refrain from anger, and forsake wrath!
> > Fret not yourself; it tends only to evil.
> *For the evildoers shall be cut off,*
> > *but those who wait for the LORD shall inherit the land.*

Holding on to grudges and contemplating revenge is an expression of no confidence in God acting righteously. Leaving room for the wrath of God is *trusting* in God. It is the obedience that derives from *faith* (Romans 1:5).

THE HUMAN EXPERIENCE OF PUSHING PAST OUR GRUDGES

Romans 12:21 says, "Do not be overcome by evil, but overcome evil with good." How do we do that? The only way I can see that it is possible to overcome evil is by laying hold of an *overwhelming* vision of the *goodness* of God. The problem is that evil is easy to see, and the more up close and personal our experience with it—such as in the case of rape, for example—the more difficult it is to see *anything* else but evil, let alone find the goodness of God. I would not believe it possible except that people have proven to me otherwise. They had to work out this salvation, this discovery of goodness, but they did come to see it and learn to wield it as a weapon till they were free.

SEEING THE GOODNESS OF GOD IN HIS COMMANDS

One place I see the goodness of God is in his law. "Your rules are good. Behold, I long for your precepts; in your righteousness give me life!" (Psalm 119:39-40). So much of what God says in his law makes sense, is so clearly good, that I am willing to trust the law in those places where it is less self-evident or so horribly inconvenient. Because I have tasted the goodness of God's ways, I will eat my peas when he says so! I will trust that the law of forgiveness is good for me and right for me and will make me happier in the long run, no matter how unpalatable loving my enemies might be at first taste.

Corrie ten Boom's struggle to forgive is well known in Christian circles, but it is worth repeating since she overcame good with evil and did so mainly by trusting in the goodness of God's commands. During World War II Corrie and her family rescued Jews from slaughter by hiding them in their house. The ten Booms were betrayed, caught, and sent to Ravensbrück concentration camp. More than 96,000 women died there, one of whom was Corrie's beloved sister, Betsie. Some years later, Corrie gave a speech at a church in Munich, after which a heavyset man approached her. Corrie recognized him as one of the most brutal guards in her camp. She froze in pain and anguish. The man said to her, "Since that time, I have become a Christian. I know that God has forgiven me for the cruel things I did there, but I would like to hear it from your lips as well. Fraulein—will you forgive me?" Corrie wrestled with what she said. It was the most difficult thing she ever did. She wrote,

> I had to do it—I knew that. The message that God forgives has a prior condition: that we forgive those who have injured us. "Jesus, help me!" I prayed silently. "I can lift my hand. I can do that much. You supply the feeling."
>
> And so woodenly, mechanically, I thrust my hand into the one stretched out to me. And as I did, an incredible thing took place. The current started in my shoulder, raced down my arm, sprang into our joined hands. And then this healing warmth seemed to flood my whole being, bringing tears to my eyes.
>
> "I forgive you, brother!" I cried. "With all my heart!"
>
> For a long moment we grasped each other's hands, the former guard and the former prisoner. I had never known God's love so intensely as I did then.[6]

I like Corrie's honesty; her account rings true. God must supply the grace to forgive. But one way he does that is through our trust in the goodness of his commands.

SEEING THE GOODNESS OF GOD IN HIS SOVEREIGNTY

Another place I see the goodness of God is in his sovereignty. The more I see it, the more I delight in it. The more I see it, the more I can trust him when the circumstances call his goodness into question. There is no greater earthly challenge to our faith in the goodness of God, in terms of our human experience, than when we are victims of evil. "Where was God? Why did he allow it?"

Heather Gemmen's story is one of home invasion, rape at knifepoint, a resulting pregnancy, a faith and marriage stretched beyond recognition, and the account of her struggle to overcome evil with good. In her moving and beautifully written account, *Startling Beauty,* she recalls how at one point her husband questioned God's sovereignty. They had long felt God had called them to live in the inner city to serve that neighborhood. At one point her husband asked, "Do you still believe that God wanted us to live here? Why? So you could get raped? If that's the case, then God is a jerk."[7]

It is the ancient, ever-present problem of pain. Before I answer how Heather answered the question, let us consider the witness of God's sovereignty in the Bible and in the life testimony of Joseph.

By ascribing sovereignty to God, we are asserting that God is not up in heaven wringing his hands, saying, "Things have gotten out of control! What am I to do?" To trust in God's sovereignty means to trust that he is in control and is working for our *good* in all things both good and *evil*. Because God is sovereign, Proverbs 16:4 can say, "The LORD has made everything for its purpose, *even the wicked* for the day of trouble." Because God is sovereign, the Bible can record how the Son of God could be "crucified and killed by the hands of lawless men" and yet declare that Jesus was "delivered up according to the definite plan and foreknowledge of God" (Acts 2:23). Sinners do wicked things and are accountable for it. God's sovereignty means that he forces even wicked behavior to serve his ultimate *good*.

God's sovereignty is declared in Romans 8:28 as a comfort to wounded believers and as the power to forgive: "We know that for those who love God *all* things work together for *good*, for those who are called according to his purpose." God is not working for good for *everyone*. For the impenitent and the obstinate, who will not turn from their wickedness, he is working out their destruction. But for those who *love God*, his outworking grace assures us that he is working for good, even in our bad, sometimes horrific experiences. Let us see if it is possible to believe such things. Let us consider how someone can endure much evil and find the goodness of God at work.

Joseph was the favorite son of the patriarch Jacob, the second youngest of twelve brothers. At one point Jacob made a richly ornamented robe for Joseph: "When his brothers saw that their father loved [Joseph] more than all his brothers, they hated him and could not speak peacefully to him" (Genesis 37:4). Favoritism, as plenty of people can testify, is a deeply painful sin and sows deep resentment in those not favored.

Joseph kindled his brothers' bitterness even more by boasting over a dream God gave him. He dreamed that one day he would actually rule over his older brothers. He saw them bowing down to him, and he *told them so* (37:5-7). Such a direct challenge to the pecking order created an insatiable desire to give Joseph his comeuppance.

One day the brothers got Joseph alone and plotted to murder him. "They said to one another, 'Here comes this dreamer. Come now, let us kill him and throw him into one of the pits. Then we will say that a fierce animal has devoured him, and we will see what will become of his dreams'" (37:19-20). At the last minute his brother Judah diverted their scheme by suggesting they sell him into slavery to a group traveling to Egypt. This had the benefit of sparing them from actual bloodguilt. They could still deceive their father into thinking Joseph was dead, and line their pockets as well. They sold Joseph into slavery, took his coat, smeared it in goat's blood, and presented it to their father, feigning deep concern: "'This we have found.' . . . [Jacob] identified it and said, 'It is my son's robe. A fierce animal has devoured him. Joseph is without doubt torn to pieces'" (Genesis 37:32-33). Jacob tore his clothes in grief, while his sons rejoiced secretly.

In Egypt, Joseph suffered the oppression of slavery for many years. Then things got *worse*. He was falsely accused of sexual harassment and attempted rape (39:1-20). Though innocent, he languished in prison for *years*.

Was God a jerk for allowing this to happen? Surely Joseph could have concluded—as many others have concluded, when all they see is evil and wickedness—that either God is impotent (not able to stop evil) or cruel and abusive ("You have treated me badly; you could have stopped this but you didn't").

Joseph was badly treated by his brothers. He was exploited as a worker, falsely accused by one he faithfully served, and subjected to barbaric conditions in prison. Through it all Joseph trusted instead in a Goodness that he could not at that time see. He trusted that God was *at work* for good. We know this because at this point in the story we are told, "[Joseph] was there in prison. *But the* LORD *was with Joseph*" (39:20-21). I take this to mean that Joseph was looking to

God and finding comfort in knowing God's presence in all his loneliness and despair.

Time passed in prison. Then two fellow prisoners had dreams, and Joseph was enabled to interpret them. Both had been employed by Pharaoh, one as a cupbearer and the other as a baker (40:1-23). The cupbearer's dream, Joseph said, promised deliverance and restoration. The thankful prisoner promised to help secure Joseph's release if the interpretation proved true. It did. Pharaoh "restored the chief cupbearer to his position, and he placed the cup in Pharaoh's hand. . . . Yet the chief cupbearer did not remember Joseph, but *forgot* him" (40:21, 23). Another *bitter* disappointment for Joseph, no doubt. Another reason to be angry; to call God a jerk and plot revenge. But Joseph trusted still in that Goodness that he could not see except through the eyes of faith.

Then Pharaoh had a disturbing dream, and suddenly the cupbearer remembered Joseph. Joseph interpreted the dream:

> God has revealed to Pharaoh what he is about to do. The seven good cows are seven years . . . [and] the seven lean and ugly cows that came up after them are seven years . . . [they are] seven years of famine (Genesis 41:25-27).

Pharaoh put Joseph in charge over all Egypt to store up food during the seven good years to bring the country through the seven years of famine. When the years of famine came, people from all over came to Egypt to buy food—even Joseph's brothers (42:1-2). So many years had passed since that awful day when they sold their own brother into slavery that they did not recognize Joseph when they stood before him, and they "bowed themselves before him with their faces to the ground" (42:6), begging to buy food. Joseph recognized them and could have taken out his revenge on the spot.

Instead, Joseph saw the sovereign guidance of God fulfilling the promise given to him in the dream he had received in his youth. He saw how God had used his own sin, his boastful arrogance, to spark an even greater and longer-term evil by his brothers. This set in motion all the other injustices that followed, that worked for still a greater good—saving his family. Joseph saw that God's good purposes not only used evil but *required* evil. Joseph said, "Do not be distressed or angry with yourselves because you sold me here, for God sent me before you to preserve life. . . . God sent me before you to preserve for you a remnant on earth, and to keep alive for you many survivors" (45:5, 7). This is the power of knowing God's sovereignty. The brothers *sold* him, but God *sent* him! This is seeing the goodness of God in his sovereignty.

When Joseph's father died, the brothers were terrified and said, "What if Joseph holds a grudge against us and pays us back for all the wrongs we did to him?" Instead of asking forgiveness, they lied again (some people just never change):

> They sent a message to Joseph, saying, "Your father gave this command before he died, 'Say to Joseph, Please forgive the transgression of your brothers and their sin, because they did evil to you.' And now, please forgive the transgression of the servants of the God of your father" (50:16-17).

Joseph's response shows the power of trusting God's sovereignty:

> Joseph wept when they spoke to him. . . . Joseph said to them, "Do not fear, for am I in the place of God? As for you, *you meant evil against me, but God meant it for good,* to bring it about that many people should be kept alive." . . . Thus he comforted them and spoke kindly to them (50:17, 19-21).

Joseph did not say they were innocent or that they had nothing to fear. He left it to God to be their judge. What he asserted was that their harmful intentions were tools in the hands of God's good intentions—to save the entire family. What Joseph could not have seen is that the famine (bad) would draw all of Jacob's family into Egypt where they would receive food (good), and that this family would grow to become a nation (good) that would be forced into four centuries of terrible bondage in Egypt (bad). In their suffering (bad) they would cry out to God (good) and be delivered by God's mighty power through Moses (good). Their deliverance as a nation laid the foundation for understanding the bondage of sin (bad) and God's deliverance from it (good) through a Savior (good). Centuries later, the Savior was crucified (bad) and gloriously resurrected (good), and is now saving many lives right down to the present time—right down to you and me. This is why we can say God is at work for good in all things, good and bad, and that, trusting in the goodness of God's sovereignty, we have the power to overcome evil with good.

Heather and her husband, working out their salvation with fear and trembling, did come to see that God was not a jerk. *Startling Beauty* is the story of how God brought them a daughter who has been the great Good brought forth from a great evil. It is a story of conquering goodness. They came to see that God was "orchestrating" good through evil and came to praise him for it. In Heather's words,

I know what you have done . . .
You stole my courage;
Your words, filthy and threatening, penetrated my soul.
I grasp in vain at a missing part of myself.

How could you not have known?
You scorned a closed door;
You scarred me with your words.
I can still feel the knife pressed against my throat.

I won't forget your laughter . . .
You who slapped me when I begged to pray,
Whose words mocked what could have set you free.
I did still pray.

And there is more that you don't know . . .
You created more than fear;
Your words are not the only thing you left behind.
I have gained more than I have lost.

Strange that I should forgive you . . .
You who do not even know you need it,

Whose words displayed your pathetic need for grace.
You didn't know what you were doing.[8]

Heather found the infusion of grace she so desperately needed. She found goodness in sovereignty. "Rape takes too much" she concludes. "But I for one, have gained more than I have lost. I have been startled by beauty in places it doesn't belong. I see it on a bloodied cross, and the bitterness loses its power. I see it on the face of the man who keeps his vows to me, and the fear releases its grip. I see it in the graceful dance of a child who was so unwanted, and hope revives its song."[9]

SEEING THE GOODNESS OF GOD IN HIS REDEEMING LOVE

And there is still more goodness to be found. Another deeply satisfying source of God's goodness is seen in his redeeming love. It provides us yet another means to conquer evil with good. This love hopes that the gospel of forgiveness and new life in Christ will win our enemies over. This love desires to see our enemies converted, not condemned, so that they become a living testimony to the glory of God's mercy in Jesus Christ.

In 1987, Michael Carlucci shot Scott Everett to death. Carlucci pleaded guilty to second-degree manslaughter and was sentenced to ten years in the state penitentiary. Scott's father, Pastor Walter Everett, in spite of his own pain, wrote a letter to Carlucci and eventually visited him. Carlucci told him that, after receiving Everett's first letter, he knelt in his prison cell and asked God for forgiveness. In prison, after an hour-long discussion, the two men stood, shook hands, embraced, and cried. Pastor Everett said, "People won't be able to understand why Jesus came and what Jesus is all about unless we forgive."[10] This is enemy-conquering goodness. After serving his time, Michael Carlucci decided to wed. Pastor Walter Everett performed the wedding ceremony for his son's killer.

Pastor Everett demonstrates that there is power in hoping for God's redeeming love to be glorified on the earth. This love can be so great, so lovely, so overwhelming that it empowers us to forgive those who have hurt us and love our enemies and do good to them. Pastor Everett's love reduced his son's killer to tears of repentance and faith in Christ. He proved the axiom "Mercy triumphs over judgment" (James 2:13). Mercy (and the forgiveness inherent in it) brings greater glory to God than judgment.

So how do we push past grudges? How do we overcome evil with good? By faith in the goodness of God. The goodness of God's commands compels us to forgive. The truth that God is always working for our good frees us from bitterness. Our hope in the conquering power of the gospel not only conquers bitterness, often it overcomes the hearts of our enemies and turns their guilt into gladness.

THE HUMAN EXPERIENCE OF GOD'S OUTWORKING GRACE

Pushing past grudges is the human experience of grace filling the soul to overflowing capacity. Such strength is found in beholding the outworking goodness of God.

GROUP STUDY QUESTIONS

1. Why do we nurse our grudges so much? What is the central problem in doing so? Why does God warn us away from bitterness in Hebrews 12:14-15?

2. In Matthew 18:21-35 Jesus teaches us why forgiving others is one of the conditions for receiving God's free grace. Why is this just and fair? How is this condition in keeping with the rule of salvation by faith alone? What is our faith trusting and depending on God for, when we forgive those who have wounded us?

3. The people we live and work with are often like sand in the eye. How can we live graciously with irritating people? Where appropriate, can you tell a story about your sand-in-the-eye experience?

4. In our learning to forgive those who have hurt us, God reminds us of his sovereignty. What are we believing when we ascribe sovereignty to God?

5. How does Joseph show us that he understood what Paul affirmed centuries later, saying, "We know that for those who love God *all* things work together for *good*, for those who are called according to his purpose" (Romans 8:28)? What "good" have you seen "working" in your trouble and sufferings?

6. What do you learn from Heather Gemmen's painful but ultimately glorious story of struggle with the wicked? What do you learn from Pastor Everett's story?

7. Whom do you need to forgive? What is your plan of action, your work done in fear and trembling, to get past the pain, anger, and resentment that has resulted? How do you plan to overcome evil with good?

10

THE GREAT WORK UNSHEATHED

Serving in the Great Work

I sometimes feel that I am living just as long as I have something great to work for.

—DIETRICH BONHOEFFER,
LETTERS AND PAPERS FROM PRISON

We are . . . created in Christ Jesus for good works, which God prepared beforehand, that we should walk in them.

—EPHESIANS 2:10

R ay entered Harvard at age fifteen *as a sophomore*, graduated at nineteen, and was a medical doctor by the time he was twenty-three. Dr. Ray Hammond, an African-American, is a godly brother and a friend. I knew he was gifted, but until I read this in the *Boston Globe*,[1] I did not know he was so singularly gifted. Why? Because I know him not as a medical doctor but as the pastor of Bethel African Methodist Episcopal Church in Boston. Dr. Hammond enjoyed a six-figure income as a surgeon on Cape Cod, but he set it all aside to start this church in his living room with his wife and four children. The mayor of Boston offered him a cabinet-level post as chief of human services. He politely refused and remains pastor of the 250-member church. What compels a man of such immense talent, for whom success, prosperity, and fame are so clearly achievable, to turn to preaching and pastoring instead among the distressed neighborhoods of Boston?

Sylvia Anthony's husband died in 1987. Before he died, the hospital supervising his care burned a hole in his stomach, making a sick man even sicker. The hospital awarded him $90,000 for its error. Being a generous man, he gave over half of it away before he died. Sylvia used a little of it to bury her husband and the rest to house young unwed mothers needing transitional housing. She opened her home and, when that filled up, rented another. In two years she had spent almost all of the money, but by then enough other people had joined in to help nurse the work along. Now called Sylvia's Haven, it provides housing for several dozen single mothers in transition. What compels a woman in her sixties, in the midst of her grief, to take the biggest chunk of money she ever saw and spend it on lost, sometimes drug-addicted and almost always rebellious young unwed mothers?

When I was a senior in high school, I put my faith in Christ. Within a year every member of my family except for my father did the same. My mother's new dedication to Christ helped her endure a difficult marriage and kept her well motivated to be an excellent and challenging public school teacher. As the work of grace unfolded, she prayed for and encouraged the family. In 1996, at age sixty-six, she found herself widowed and retired. She called to tell me she was moving to *Russia* as a missionary! She bore the harsh winters of Nizhny Novgorod (Gorky) to teach Christian ethics and morality in the public schools to teachers, students, and their parents. After several years, she spent *only* about five months a year there, helping in a variety of evangelistic activities. In the summer of 2005, she announced on her seventy-fifth birthday that, sadly, her time in Russia was over. She felt God calling her to serve in Mongolia! She left for her new ministry that fall. Is she daft? Or is there something about the outworking of God's grace that compels us into great works of love?

RECIPIENTS OF THE GOSPEL BECOME SERVANTS OF THE GOSPEL

Ray, Sylvia, and my mother demonstrate how every recipient of the gospel becomes a servant of the gospel; it is part of the work of grace. The apostle Paul wrote, "Of this gospel I was *made a minister* according to the gift of God's grace, which was given me *by the working of his power*" (Ephesians 3:7-8). The grace of God calls us to repentance and faith, produces a panting heart for God, then commissions us to a life of service in a broken world. We breathe in salvation and we exhale servanthood.

"Do not be slothful in zeal, be fervent in spirit, *serve* the Lord" (Romans 12:11). "Through love *serve* one another" (Galatians 5:13). It is something love compels us to do, as 1 Peter 5:2 says, "not under compulsion, but willingly, as God would have you; not for shameful gain, but eagerly." Servanthood is a way of life among the forgiven. Charles Swindoll calls it "the art of unselfish living."[2] That is because the new focus of our life is to love God and our neighbor.

Serving God becomes the *purpose* of our life, because that is part of the purpose of grace. "How much more will the blood of Christ . . . purify our conscience from dead works *to serve the living God*" (Hebrews 9:14). We began as guilty sinners, living empty lives, and through the sanctifying power of his Spirit and belief in the truth, God washes, heals, molds, and spurs us on to a place where we wake up every day of our lives with the highest of all purposes for getting out of bed. We serve the living God!

Let us return one last time to our anchor text and notice how gloriously far the gospel takes us: from being a guilty sinner to being a servant of God:

> And you, who once were alienated and hostile in mind, doing evil deeds, he has now reconciled in his body of flesh by his death, in order to present you holy and blameless and above reproach before him, if indeed you continue in the faith, stable and steadfast, not shifting from the hope of the gospel that you heard, which has been proclaimed in all creation under heaven, *and of which I, Paul, became a minister* (Colossians 1:21-23).

The Great Work takes the hostile and turns them into partners in the ministry of the gospel. It is an indictment of the feeble and anemic preaching of the age that folks like Ray Hammond, Sylvia Anthony, or my mother should be extraordinary at all. They represent normative Christianity in the outworking of God's grace. It is not the Spirit of *grace* that for so many has made comfort and retirement the end of Christian faith; it is the Spirit of the age gone unchallenged. When grace is at work and on the move, cross-bearing in hard places, fed by the secret spring of joy in a better world yet to be realized, is found in its wake.

SERVING GOD MEANS FINDING SOMETHING GOOD TO DO

I asked Sylvia Anthony when she first thought about opening her home to unwed mothers. She said, "From the moment I became a Christian, I wanted to serve God; I just wasn't sure how. Then I heard about how young mothers needed places to stay in order to keep their babies, and I just knew I had to do something." Sylvia's experience of God's grace is the authentic Christian experience. By grace her sins were forgiven and by grace she turned her focus outward and looked for something good to do.

God has ordained for each of us something good to do. "We are . . . created in Christ Jesus for *good works,* which God prepared beforehand, that we should walk in them" (Ephesians 2:10). "[Christ] gave himself for us to redeem us from all lawlessness and to purify for himself a people for his own possession who are *zealous for good works"* (Titus 2:14).

SERVING A GOD NOT SERVED BY HUMAN HANDS

These works of service are not done because God cannot get things done without us, as if he has a need that we are meeting. God has no such need. "The God who made the world and everything in it, being Lord of heaven and earth, does not live in temples made by man, *nor is he served by human hands, as though he needed anything,* since he himself gives to all mankind life and breath and everything" (Acts 17:24-25). This is so contrary to that motivational speech that says, "Let's get out there. God needs us. We are God's hands and feet!" God is not served by human hands! He has no needs. He holds the very idea of it up to ridicule:

> "I will not accept a bull from your house
>> or goats from your folds.
> For every beast of the forest is mine,
>> the cattle on a thousand hills.
> I know all the birds of the hills,
>> and all that moves in the field is mine.
> If I were hungry, I would not tell you,
>> for the world and its fullness are mine.
> Do I eat the flesh of bulls
>> or drink the blood of goats?
> Offer to God a sacrifice of thanksgiving,
>> and perform your vows to the Most High,
> and call upon me in the day of trouble;
>> I will deliver you, and you shall glorify me" (Psalm 50:9-15).

God has no need to be served; we have a need to serve. God gives me work to do in the same way I gave a paintbrush to my son when he was small. Since he loved his dad, he wanted to do what Dad did. He wanted to paint *with* Dad and climb the ladder *like* Dad and have his picture taken *beside* Dad in front of the house when it was done. Dad could have painted the house all by himself, and done it more quickly and better. But Dad enjoys his son and is pleased by the son's desire to imitate him. So, being his dad, I brought him out to see what was going on and calculated the minutes till he would ask, "Can I paint too?" At first my hand overlaid his as he brushed on the paint. I taught and directed him what to do. I held him steady on the ladder.

So it is with our good works. God is working in and through us. In practice this means serving with a conscious *dependence* on God to supply the wisdom and power needed for the work and doing it with a conscious *desire* to advance the glory of God's name—not ours—in the world. This is the meaning of 1 Peter 4:11: "whoever serves, as one who serves *by the strength that God supplies*—in order that in everything God may be glorified through Jesus Christ."

OUR GOOD WORKS ARE PART OF HIS GREAT WORK

The German pastor Dietrich Bonhoeffer, arrested and eventually executed for his opposition to Hitler, wrote from his cell, "I sometimes feel that I am living just as long as I have something great to work for."[3] What makes it so exciting to serve God is that our good works are a contributing part to his Great Work.

God's Great Work is ever penetrating into the human experience, yet global in scope, and expanding through the ages of time. Stephen W. Hawking, in his book *A Brief History of Time,* attempts an intriguing unified theory of space and time. Einstein's theory of relativity pointed to an ever-expanding universe, tracked now by cosmic background radiation. By definition an expanding universe points to an explosive beginning point of seemingly infinite compression of matter. Quantum mechanics is the study of the universe within the single atom. "Atom" means indivisible. It was once thought to be the smallest building block of matter. Then we discovered the subatomic particles of neutrons, protons, and electrons, spinning in their own subatomic universe. In recent years, theoretical physicists have talked of protons and neutrons displaying internal structure, meaning they are made of still smaller parts, called quarks.

Tracking back toward the expanse of the heavens, physicists speak of black holes, dark matter, quasars, and more. Quasars are the brightest objects of the universe. They are ultra-luminous cores of young galaxies, perhaps up to a hundred whole *galaxies* clustered together by unknown forces, condensed in a region the size of our own solar system, thus explaining their brightness. In the same way, God is doing an infinitely glorious work in one life, touching body and soul, joint and marrow, mind and spirit. The broad sketches of that penetrating work have been the outline of this book. But God is doing this work of grace on a grand and global time/space continuum. It is for all time and is expanding into every place.

A few weeks after I became a Christian at seventeen, I was sitting in church and an older gentleman stood up to lead the congregation in an evening prayer. In his prayer, he praised God for his faithfulness that he had personally experienced the past thirty years. I sat there amazed, thinking, *God, this thing you are doing in me, you have been doing it a long time now. Thirty years!* I was awakening to the reality that trusting in Christ brought me into something historic and global—something far greater than I first realized. I had stumbled upon the Great Work.

FROM QUARKS TO QUASARS IN THE GREAT WORK

God's Great Work was conceived before the creation of the world (Ephesians 1:4). It was first revealed when God declared to Abraham his intention to launch an international global movement birthed out of a nation of people not yet born:

> "And *I will make of you a great nation,* and I will bless you and make your name great, so that you will be a blessing. I will bless those who bless you, and him who dishonors you I will curse, and in you *all the families of the earth* shall be blessed" (Genesis 12:2-3).

Through Abraham, God would build a nation, and then through that nation God would so work that *all the peoples on earth* would be made glad of heart (blessed). Centuries later, King David, now leader of the very nation God had promised to create, worshiped God in anticipation of the gladdening that would flow from Israel into the river of every nation and the rivulet of every people group in those nations:

> . . . that your way may be known on earth,
> your saving power among all *nations.*
> Let the peoples praise you, O God;
> let all the peoples praise you!
> *Let the nations be glad and sing for joy* (Psalm 67:2-4).

When Jesus came, he commissioned us to serve under his own authority in the global advancement of this Great Work:

"All authority in heaven and on earth has been given to me. Go therefore and make disciples of all *nations,* baptizing them in the name of the Father and of the Son and of the Holy Spirit, teaching them to observe all that I have commanded you. And behold, I am with you always, to the end of the age" (Matthew 28:18-20).[4]

We live in the rising sunlight of the approaching completion of the Great Work. By trusting in Christ personally, we bring the Great Work one step closer to fulfillment. We advance the Great Work by the power of a godly life and the good works produced by our faith. As we do so, others move from guilt to gladness, till all the rest of God's elect hear and respond and cross over from death to life. By the time the Great Work is completed, people from every tribe and tongue on earth will testify to a heart made glad in the work of God's grace, through their faith in Jesus Christ. Revelation 7:9-10 gives us a picture of the Great Work completed:

> After this I looked, and behold, a great multitude that no one could number, from every nation, from all tribes and peoples and languages, standing before the throne and before the Lamb, clothed in white robes, with palm branches in their hands, and crying out with a loud voice, "Salvation belongs to our God who sits on the throne, and to the Lamb!"

THE GREATEST WORLD MOVEMENT IN HISTORY

The spectacular advancement of God's Great Work is visible by tracing out the growth of the church. After Christ ascended, almost the entire church assembled in a single upper room (Acts 1:12-14). By the end of the lives of those first believers, the movement had penetrated the major cities of the known world. By A.D. 100, Christians constituted a tiny 0.5 percent of the world population. It took another 1,400 years to hit the 1 percent mark (circa 1430). It took only 360 years more, however, to hit 2 percent of the world population (1790) and only 150 years to move to 3 percent, which occurred around 1940. In the last 50 years the world Christian movement has grown to 11 percent of the world's population, gaining a percentage point every 2 to 3 years![5]

Ralph Winter writes, "Despite the rapid increase of world population, Christianity is simply growing faster than any other global religion when what is measured is its most relevant type of growth—the growth of committed adherents."[6] According to the best and most conservative estimates, 82,000 people come to Christ every day![7] In China, 23,000 are added daily. In Africa, 16,000. More people have turned to Christ in the last decade from the Muslim world than in the last millennium. Why is this happening? Because Christ said, "This gospel . . . will be proclaimed throughout the whole world as a testimony to all nations, and then the end will come" (Matthew 24:14). The Great Work is a worldwide work—at least it will be before it is completed.

RESISTANCE AND SUFFERING IN THE GREAT WORK

Concerning this Great Work Christ said, "I will build my church, and the gates of hell shall not prevail against it" (Matthew 16:18). This does not mean that there is no resistance. The gates of hell resist! But they do not succeed. As we work to relieve suffering, the gospel wins hearts. When we are called to endure suffering, the gospel wins still more hearts!

The Great Work of the gospel has advanced in spite of steady and sometimes deadly opposition. According to David Barrett, author of the *World Christian Encyclopedia,* more people have suffered imprisonment, torture, and death for their service to the gospel in the last hundred years than in all previous centuries put together. In Herbert Schlossberg's aptly named book *Called to Suffer, Called to Triumph,* he explores the terrible opposition Christians have faced in China, for example. The Cultural Revolution (1966–1976) was especially hard on the church, with Christianity equated with foreign and anti-communist ways.

Schlossberg tells about Pastor Kwan Ying. In 1979, Ying climbed down from a train in Beijing to greet his family. "My heart pounded as I spied my family walking my way . . . and then right past me. They hadn't recognized me. And no wonder—it had been fifteen years since we had seen each other." Kwan spent twenty-one years in prison for being a Christian and refusing to stop acting like one. But during that time, what happened? After the Cultural Revolution, information gradually seeped out that showed astonishing vitality in the repressed church, so that best estimates put the number of believers in China at over 50 million.[8] After seventy years of communism, in which God was "deleted" from the minds of the people, the wall fell, and behold, 36 percent of Russia was Christian. The church had five times the membership of the Communist Party. In the words of Earle Cairns, the stories of God's Great Work form "an endless line of splendor."[9]

The conquering power of the gospel has faced as much danger from within the church as from without. Moral and theological corruption has done much to scandalize the gospel and impede its progress in the hearts of men and women. The darkest moment of church history came when we perverted the gospel and tried to advance by the sword rather than the winsome power of good works. The sad effects of the Crusades linger to this day. Even so, God brought reform and renewal, as he constantly does. And when he does, the Great Work surges forward, abolishing slavery, creating universities, expanding art and science and medicine through the work of people now living for the glory of God.[10]

HOW DO I FIND MY PART IN THE GREAT WORK?

It is not uncommon for us to struggle a long time trying to discern God's will for our lives. But one part of the answer is relatively easy and freeing. The Great Work boils down in practice to doing the works that *love* prompts us to do. The apostle Paul called it our "labor of love" (1 Thessalonians 1:3). Your part in the Great Work is what God's love at work in you prompts you to do. If you will live in the love of God, he will lead you through the promptings of love to many good works of service.

Jesus told the parable of the Good Samaritan (Luke 10:25-37) to illustrate how our part in the Great Work is fulfilled by simply obeying the promptings of love. A Samaritan saw a man beaten, stripped naked, and left for dead. He was able to fulfill the law of God by simply following the demands of love. He picked the man up, bandaged his wounds, took him to an inn, and paid for his care. Ralph Waldo Emerson said, "Give all to love, obey thy heart."[11] This is the biblical pattern, and for centuries it has worked as a guide for serving in the Great Work of God.

The law of love prompted the Hebrew midwives to rescue babies from death in Pharaoh's day (Exodus 1:16-20). Obadiah provided food and shelter for a hundred prophets in the days of Jezebel (1 Kings 18:4). Psalm 82:3-4 says,

> Give justice to the weak and the fatherless;
>   maintain the right of the afflicted and the destitute.
> Rescue the weak and the needy;
>   deliver them from the hand of the wicked.

The outworking of God's grace does not reach its end in our private reformation. It works outward toward the public good. It is the law of love at work *in us* for the sake of others. The law of love picks a fight with poverty and oppression and darkness. It produces entrepreneurs of grace and virtue capitalists. It fights a war of love against all things that destroy body and soul. In the process, some are able to shut the mouths of lions while others are sawn in two (Hebrews 11:32, 37). The law of love risks and sacrifices and suffers and weeps and yet rejoices. The law of love obeyed leads to radical joy in God and a muscular Christianity in the world. Where the law of love is obeyed, Matthew 25:35-36 says, the sick are cared for, not euthanized. The imprisoned are visited, not left to despair in their guilt. The immigrant is assisted, not despised. The thirsty are given a glass of water. Is it not amazing that fetching water can be one of the good works God has prepared in advance that we should do? Love should lead some of us men to befriend the neighbor boy who has no dad. Love should lead some to check in on the elderly woman who has lost her husband and perhaps fix her faucet.

Love invented the piggy bank! It was originally created by mission societies as a fundraising method to provide missionaries in China with funds for buying piglets. And why were the missionaries there? Love prompted them to leave their own neighborhood and adopt a new one so that the gladness of the gospel could spread to the nations. Love led the early missionaries to Africa to pack their belongings in *coffins* because they had such a short life expectancy. Tropical diseases generally claimed their lives within a year of arriving on the mission field. Medical missions began in an effort to prolong the lives of missionaries. Why? Because we loved them and the people they went to serve. Love has started many schools. Eighty-five percent of the schools in Africa today were started by Christians.[12] What has happened as a result? In 1900, Africa was 4 percent Christian. Today 40 percent of the people of Africa identify themselves as Christian. Good works, prompted by love, produce a Great Work.

Love prompted a presidential resignation in order to take up bedpans. Dr. Robertson McQuilkin was doing a good work in the Great Work. He was the president of Columbia Bible College and Seminary in Columbia, South Carolina. This school has a worldwide ministry and a multimillion-dollar budget. In 1990 his wife was stricken with Alzheimer's disease. For several years, with extra help, he was able to serve both the college and his wife. But the law of love told him when it was time to resign his highly respected worldwide ministry to care for his wife through "her brave descent into oblivion":

> When the time came, the decision was firm. It took no great calculation. It was a matter of integrity. Had I not promised, 42 years before, "in sickness and in health . . . till death do us part"?
>
> This was no grim duty to which I was stoically resigned, however. It was only fair. She had, after all, cared for me for almost four decades with marvelous devotion; now it was my turn. And such a partner she was! If I took care of her for 40 years, I would never be out of her debt. . . .
>
> Resignation was painful; but the right path was not difficult to discern.[13]

Do you see how loving God and neighbors, more than golf and new houses, is the power of God's grace unsheathed? Loving God will lead some of us to pack our mittens and head for Moscow. It will lead some to open their spare bedroom to an unwed mother in pregnancy distress. It will lead some of us to serve the disadvantaged in our urban neighborhoods. But it will lead all of us who love Jesus and long for his appearing to say with Mary, "I am the *servant* of the Lord" (Luke 1:38), and then go find something *good* to do.

The Human Experience of God's Outworking Grace

Serving God, by serving in his Great Work of bringing the gospel's love, truth, and mercy to the world around us, is the Christian's fountain of youth. It keeps us ever young in the gladness of God and ever hopeful for the spread of his glory.

GROUP STUDY QUESTIONS

1. According to Titus 2:14, what new zeal results from God's outworking grace? How have you experienced this? What has it prompted you to do?
2. What people in your life or people that you have come to learn about exemplify a life of service to God?
3. In what way can serving God be demeaning to God, according to Paul in Acts 17:24-25? How does Peter instruct us, in 1 Peter 4:11, to serve God in a way that honors and glorifies his power and purposes in the world?
4. What are some of the ways we can serve the living God? Survey Psalm 82; Isaiah 58; Matthew 25:31-46; 1 Corinthians 12; James 1:27.
5. What stories in your life reflect the parable of the Good Samaritan? What have you enjoyed doing or sacrificed to do, because you were prompted by love?
6. Would you like to tell me about how the Great Work has affected you? You may e-mail me at: contactjohn@johnensor.org.

A FINAL
THOUGHT

As we have seen, the human experience of God's outworking grace takes us far beyond just a desire for forgiveness. But it is all connected with forgiveness, leading to and flowing from it. It is all part of "Christ and him crucified." The more clearly we see those connections, the more firmly and boldly will we live out the call of God on our lives. The pull of contemporary expectations and the drag of our own spiritual laziness are against us. Let us work out the grace of God, our salvation, knowing that God is at work in us for this same purpose.

And let us not grow weary in this work, no matter how hard life becomes or what "frowning providences" we must endure. Surely we must learn to fight patiently through our discouragement when we are confronted with our own waning zeal. The lusts within us have many of their own resurrections. Let us persevere in faith. And let us rejoice in the ongoing outworking of God's grace and look forward to its completion. This is our hope:

> Always in every prayer of mine for you all making my prayer with *joy,*
> because of your partnership in the gospel from the first day until now.
> And I am sure of this, that he who began a good work in you will
> bring it to completion at the day of Jesus Christ (Philippians 1:4-6)

"The day of Jesus Christ" will be a grand day. It signals the *completion* of the war against our flesh, the world, and the Devil and the *consummation* of our happiness in the holiness of God. Let us hold fast to this hope and hold it gladly! It is the hope of glory.

NOTES

INTRODUCTION

1. Alexander Pope, *An Essay on Criticism* (I.i.9).
2. John R. W. Stott, *The Cross of Christ* (Downers Grove, Ill.: InterVarsity Press, 1986), 88.
3. Cited in Gordon S. Jackson, compiler, *Quotes for the Journey, Wisdom for the Way* (Colorado Springs: NavPress, 2000), 73.
4. Henri Nouwen, cited in Bob Benson and Michael W. Benson, *Disciplines of the Inner Life* (Waco, Tex.: Word, 1985), 30.
5. The expression "a severe mercy" is from the title of Sheldon Vanauken's book, *A Severe Mercy* (San Francisco: Harper & Row, 1977).

CHAPTER 1: THE GREAT WORK CONSIDERED

1. Cited in John R. W. Stott, *The Cross of Christ* (Downers Grove, Ill.: InterVarsity Press, 1986), 87.
2. Fyodor Dostoyevsky, *The Brothers Karamazov*, trans. Constance Garnett (New York: New American Library, 1957), 226.
3. Jonathan Edwards, "Dissertation Concerning the End for Which God Created the World," in *The Works of Jonathan Edwards*, 2 vols. (Edinburgh: Banner of Truth, 1974), 1:94.
4. Dana Olson, unpublished ordination paper, 1-2. Used by permission.
5. Cited in Richard Cecil, "Memoirs of the Author," in John Newton, *The Works of the Rev. John Newton*, 6 vols. (Edinburgh: Banner of Truth, 1985), 1:90.

CHAPTER 2: THE GREAT WORK DESIRED

1. Plutarch, *Lives*, "Demetrius," sec. 1.
2. C. S. Lewis, *Surprised by Joy* (New York: Harcourt, Brace & World, 1955), 227.
3. Nietzsche said, "What is more harmful than any vice" is "active sympathy for the ill-constituted and weak—Christianity" (cited in John R. W. Stott, *The Cross of Christ* [Downers Grove, Ill.: InterVarsity Press, 1986], 43).
4. Ole Hallesby, *Conscience*, trans. C. J. Carlsen (London: InterVarsity, 1950), 9.
5. William K. Kilpatrick, *Psychological Seduction: The Failure of Modern Psychology* (Ridgefield, Conn.: McCaffrey, 1983), 36.
6. In some modern hymnals, the word *worm* has been replaced with *sinners*. I suspect that this is because *worm* runs contrary to contemporary theories on self-esteem.
7. George MacDonald, "The Wise Woman, or the Lost Princess," in *The Gifts of the Child Christ: Fairytales and Stories for the Childlike*, 2 vols. (Grand Rapids, Mich.: Eerdmans, 1973), 1:202.
8. Frederick Buechner, cited in Larry Crabb, *Men and Women: Enjoying the Difference* (Grand Rapids, Mich.: Zondervan, 1991), 25.
9. Larry Crabb, at a conference I attended, illustrated the problem of self-centeredness in marriage, saying, "We got two ticks here and no dog!"
10. Lewis, *Surprised by Joy*, 226.
11. H. R. Mackintosh, *The Christian Experience of Forgiveness* (London: Nisbet, 1927), 9.
12. Lewis, *Surprised by Joy*, 229.

CHAPTER 3: THE GREAT WORK NEEDED

1. Robert Murray McCheyne, "God's Rectitude in Future Punishment," in *Sermons of Robert Murray McCheyne* (Edinburgh: Banner of Truth, 1961), 177.

2. Cited in Gordon S. Jackson, compiler, *Quotes for the Journey, Wisdom for the Way* (Colorado Springs: NavPress, 2000), 66.

3. This example raises the question, are there degrees of sin? Are not some sins worse than others? Is not the murder of Vera worse than my stealing? The biblical answer appears to be yes in one sense, and no in another. All sin is the same and yet different in the sense that acorns and oak trees are the same and yet different. All sin, and each sin, from the slightest to the greatest, is a no-confidence vote in the goodness and trustworthiness of God. In this sense there is no difference between murder and murmuring; they are different *sins* that point to one eternally sinful sin: believing God is not trustworthy to be my very great delight! Murmuring is God-hatred in the acorn stage. Murder is God-hatred in the oak tree stage.

Jesus taught us that all sins are the same in this sense when he said,

"You have heard that it was said to those of old, 'You shall not murder; and whoever murders will be liable to judgment.' But I say to you that everyone who is angry with his brother will be liable to judgment; whoever insults his brother will be liable to the council; and whoever says, 'You fool!' will be liable to the hell of fire" (Matthew 5:21-22).

The reason that name-calling is a sin worthy of the fire of hell is because it is an expression of debasement for a human being made in the image of God, for the glory of God. It is a form of defacement of God's own property. Murder is the same hatred, only expressed in a far greater degree of defacement. They are the same in kind (both a form of hatred) but different in degree. Calling a man a jerk is murder in the acorn stage. Murder is hatred matured to the fullest degree.

There certainly are degrees of sin, though, in terms of the pain and devastation it causes. An acorn and an oak tree may be the same in one sense, but I would very much prefer an acorn to fall on my head than an oak tree! I would certainly prefer someone to call me a jerk than to shoot me. There are degrees of maturity in evil. The more understanding we have of a moral obligation, the more evil it is to defy that obligation. So murder reflects a greater hardness of heart against the glory of God, because people generally know the obligation not to kill. In our courts, our sense of justice causes us to give different penalties depending on the degree of damage the act causes our fellow man or the degree of defiance against the social good it reflects, or the degree of moral light the accused had. In this sense there are degrees of sin. For speeding we get a ticket. For drunk driving we get jail time, especially if someone else is hurt or killed. For running down the boss for not promoting us, we get life in prison or the death penalty. The greater the degree of defiance and rebellion to the known good, the greater punishment justice demands. The same is true of everlasting punishment. God judges the defacement of his glory by the amount of light (sense of moral duty) a person has received (Romans 2:12-24). For examples, see Matthew 10:15; 11:20-24; Luke 12:47-48; John 19:11.

4. W. G. T. Shedd, *The Doctrine of Eternal Punishment* (Edinburgh: Banner of Truth, 1986), 12-13.

5. There are some who do not believe that hell is eternal and penal in nature. They argue that *eternal punishment* does not mean punishment that is eternal. They suggest that at some point the wicked cease to exist. I fear this is wishful thinking. In Matthew 25:46, Jesus clearly draws an evenhanded picture; we will be judged worthy to receive either eternal life or eternal punishment. The word *eternal* is applied to both, and I have never read anyone argue that eternal life does not mean being alive in God's presence forever. In addition, the punishment of hell, Jesus says elsewhere, is "the unquenchable fire" (Mark 9:43), a place where the "worm does not die and the fire is not quenched" (Mark 9:48). Further indication that God's wrath, according to Jesus, does not involve being annihilated at some point, so that we cease to exist, is

found in the damnation of Judas: "Woe to that man by whom the Son of Man is betrayed! It would have been better for that man if he had not been born" (Matthew 26:24). I take this to mean that Judas would welcome a state of nonexistence, such as he had before he was born, but will not find it. For further study, see Robert Peterson, *Hell on Trial* (Phillipsburg, N.J.: Presbyterian & Reformed, 1995).

6. As we will learn, moral goodness, according to the Bible, refers to what we do out of our personal relationship with God, through our faith in Christ, for the glory of his name (Romans 14:6; Acts 17:31).

7. It is possible that the preacher was thinking of a text such as Ezekiel 33:11: "As I live, declares the Lord GOD, I have no pleasure in the death of the wicked, but that the wicked turn from his way and live." However, his attempt to reflect this sentiment does not adequately explain a text such as Deuteronomy 28:63: "The LORD will take delight in bringing ruin upon you and destroying you." I explain a better way to understand the truthfulness of both of these sentiments in chapter 4, pages 71-73.

CHAPTER 4: THE GREAT WORK PROMISED

1. Charles Simeon, cited in John R. W. Stott, *Evangelical Preaching: An Anthology of Sermons by Charles Simeon* (Portland, Ore.: Multnomah, 1986), xxxv.

2. Søren Kierkegaard, *Fear and Trembling and the Sickness unto Death,* trans. Walter Lowrie (Princeton, N.J.: Princeton University Press, 1968), 154. This death, Kierkegaard went on to describe, is *eternal* in nature:

   Thus it is that despair, this sickness in the self, is the sickness unto death. The despairing man is mortally ill. In an entirely different sense than can appropriately be said of any disease, we may say that the sickness has attacked the noblest part; and yet the man cannot die. Death is not the last phase of the sickness, but death is *continually* the last. To be delivered from this sickness by death is an impossibility, for the sickness and its torment . . . and death consist in not being able to die.

   This is a stunning description of the torments of hell.

3. Child-sacrifice, according to the Bible, represents the highest expression of contempt for God and his glory (see Leviticus 20:2-5; Deuteronomy 12:31). Perhaps the clearest expression of God's outrage over child-sacrifice is recorded in Ezekiel 16:20-21, where God explains why he did not forgive the Israelites: "And you took your sons and your daughters, whom you had borne to me, and these you sacrificed to them [that is, to false gods] to be devoured. Were your whorings so small a matter that you slaughtered my children and delivered them up as an offering by fire to them?" I developed this and its implications for abortion elsewhere. See John Ensor, *Answering the Call: Saving Innocent Lives, One Woman at a Time* (Colorado Springs: Focus on the Family, 2003).

4. Cited in Peter Masters, *Men of Destiny,* rev. ed. (London: Wakeman, 1989), 91.

5. Ibid., 96.

6. Daniel P. Fuller, *The Unity of the Bible* (Grand Rapids, Mich.: Zondervan, 1992), 196.

CHAPTER 5: THE GREAT WORK REVEALED

1. The very first promise of a coming rescuer was given in Genesis 3:15.

2. Jesus did not come to rescue everybody, or everybody would be rescued through his complete work on the cross. He came to "save *his people* from their sins" (Matthew 1:21). "His people" are those who repent and put their faith in him. "'And a Redeemer will come to Zion, to those in Jacob who turn from transgression,' declares the LORD" (Isaiah 59:20; see also Galatians 3:26). When the angels appeared to the shepherds, they shouted, "Glory to God in the highest, and on earth peace among those *with whom he is pleased!*" (Luke 2:14).

His peace is not on everyone, but on those with whom he is *pleased*. And with whom is he pleased? He is pleased with those who repent and put their hope in him (see chapter 4). He fiercely *opposes* the rest. Jesus used the metaphor of the shepherd and the sheep to explain the scope of his mission. The shepherd "calls his *own* sheep by name and leads them out . . . the sheep *follow* him, for they know his voice" (John 10:3-4). Then he applied this to himself and the people he came to rescue: "I am the good shepherd. I know *my own* and my own know me, just as the Father knows me and I know the Father; and I lay down my life for the sheep" (10:14-15). If you ask who are Jesus' sheep, it is those who *hear his voice and follow him*. The rest, who refuse his call, are not his sheep and will remain under the wrath of God.

When Jesus was about to lay down his life on the cross, he prayed for those he had come to rescue. It is not everybody in the whole world: "I am not praying for the world but *for those whom you have given me*, for they are yours" (John 17:9). When you ask who the Father has *given* to the Son to purchase forgiveness for and give eternal life, the answer again is not everybody, but those who *believe*, shown by their *obedience* to God's Word. "Yours they were, and you gave them to me, and they have kept your word . . . and have come to know in truth that I came from you; and they have believed that you sent me" (John 17:6, 8).

The biblical and theological word for those included in Christ's rescue mission is the *elect* (Matthew 24:22-31; Romans 11:7; 2 Timothy 2:10). The distinguishing mark of the elect is *faith* in Christ—repentant, obedient, persevering, joyful faith. We grow in confidence that we are among the elect as we grow in this faith, for that is how the elect *prove* they are the elect (2 Peter 1:3-11, esp. v. 10).

3. In contrast, social and economic standing more often than not mask true spiritual poverty. Wealth and influence ought not have any relevance as to how we view ourselves before God, but it does. It hinders honest self-examination. Wealth and power provide remarkable freedom and opportunity to buy and go and do as we please. The sins that the rich and powerful are most susceptible to therefore have to do with dealing unjustly with laborers, living a life of self-indulgence, ignoring the needs of the poor, and turning a deaf ear to the cries of the oppressed.

"Come now, you rich, weep and howl for the miseries that are coming upon you" (James 5:1). The rich, too, are under the wrath of God: "Your riches have rotted and your garments are moth-eaten" (5:2). All the luxuries of wealth are as filthy rags (Isaiah 64:6, NIV) before God: "Behold, the wages of the laborers who mowed your fields, which you kept back by fraud, are crying out against you" (5:4). Where power and wealth have led to the abuse and exploitation of others, there will be a harsh accounting: "You have lived on the earth in luxury and in self-indulgence. You have fattened your hearts in a day of slaughter" (5:5). If you are prosperous and have no need, you are still in need of repentance and a miracle to escape the just judgments of the Lord: "Let the lowly brother boast in his exaltation, and the rich in his humiliation, because like a flower of the grass he will pass away. . . . So also will the rich man fade away in the midst of his pursuits" (James 1:9, 11).

4. Blaise Pascal, *The Mind on Fire: The Anthology of the Writings of Blaise Pascal*, ed. James M. Houston (Portland, Ore.: Multnomah, 1989), 164.

5. Jonathan Edwards, "The Excellency of Christ," in *The Works of Jonathan Edwards*, 2 vols. (Edinburgh: Banner of Truth, 1974), 1:687.

CHAPTER 6: THE GREAT WORK JUSTIFIED

1. Cited in Lance Gay, "Auschwitz Survivors Pay Tribute to Victims," *Boston Herald*, January 27, 1995, 3. Some may think such a prayer is cold or wicked. It might be. Such prayers can be. But I think Dr. Wiesel's prayer is rooted in a deep sense of divine justice. He knows that God must act justly or show a great contempt for the people he created in his image that were so degraded and so many of whom were slaughtered; and in some way, to some degree, he senses God's own glory demeaned here as well.

We find similar prayers in the Bible. For example, Jeremiah prayed for relief against his oppressors:

Yet you, O LORD, know
all their plotting to kill me.
Forgive not their iniquity,
nor blot out their sin from your sight (Jeremiah 18:23).

2. Martin Hengel, *Crucifixion,* trans. John Bowden (Philadelphia: Fortress, 1977), 22, 25.

3. Jacqueline Syrup Bergan and S. Marie Schwan, *Forgiveness: A Guide for Prayer* (Winona, Minn.: Saint Mary's Press, 1985), 15-16.

4. How is it that such a short though intense period of suffering can fully pay the eternal debt I owe for my evil behavior? How can three days of suffering pay for an eternity of condemnation for all of God's people? I do not know. My mind overheats when I try to grasp it from that angle. But I do know the suffering Christ endured as our complete atonement did not start with his betrayal and arrest, crucifixion and burial. It was only consummated there. From the moment Christ was conceived of the virgin Mary, he suffered the immeasurable loss of glory and took up our humiliation and shame:

who, though he was in the form of God, did not count equality with God a thing to be grasped, *but made himself nothing, taking the form of a servant,* being born in the likeness of men (Philippians 2:6-7).

Contemplate the painful loss of glory, majesty, power, and union Jesus had enjoyed with the Father. In being born, he died to it all and became *nothing* and a *servant* to sinful man.

Imagine the pain of losing all your human abilities and liberties if one day you humbled yourself to become a poodle. The humiliation and frustration would be intense and immediate. Now you cannot see over anything more than two feet tall. You cannot lift anything except with your mouth. You cannot hold a pen to write a love letter. You cannot hold a nail to build a house. You cannot cook a Thanksgiving meal. You now eat hard, dry cereal or mushy, canned mystery meat every day. You drink only water, which you must lap with your tongue. You must sleep in the corner, moan at the door whenever you have to relieve yourself, and then do it outside in the open. Every time you want to say something, the same sound comes out of your mouth, more or less. And your essential value and admiration come in direct proportion to how well you meet the needs of humans, as their servant. In the same way, only infinitely greater in degree, Christ suffered the loss of all his glory as God in humbling himself to be a man and then a servant to sinful men.

Then his suffering increased. He suffered poverty and lack of comfort from the moment he was born in a cowshed (Luke 2:7). He was targeted for destruction by Herod, so that his parents had to take him and flee to Egypt (Matthew 2:13). He suffered the knowledge that his birth had resulted in the death of every potential playmate he might have known in his hometown. For every male child under two was slaughtered (Matthew 2:16-18). Consider the stares of women his mother's age that he must have endured upon his return to the area.

Further, he suffered the loss of all his divine prerogatives and grew up as a simple carpenter, making his living "by the sweat of [his] brow" (see Genesis 3:19, NIV). When he did publicly show his glory, he suffered the intense shame and humiliation of being judged a glutton and a drunkard (Matthew 11:19). We all know how hard it is to endure a false accusation! Consider how much worse it was for Christ. He is all Truth, yet he was called a deceiver (John 7:12). He possessed the mind of God but was considered a madman (John 10:20). If you can sense how painful this was to endure, remember that the charge did not come from his enemies only. His own family thought he was "out of his mind" (Mark 3:21).

Christ was accused of being demonic and a blasphemer of the very God whose name he came to glorify (Luke 5:21). Christ suffered this reproach everywhere he went and even survived numerous assassination attempts (Matthew 2:13; 12:14; 26:4).

Finally, he was betrayed by one he had befriended for three years and was sold to his assassins for thirty pieces of gold, the price of a slave (Mark 14:41).

Having all his divine glory rejected, he then suffered the loss of his dignity as a man—stripped naked, spat upon, degraded, and mocked. Finally, he suffered the cross. But take note that it was not the same kind of death that martyrs suffer. Martyrs face death with the peace of God coursing through their veins, strengthening their hearts. When Stephen was seized and falsely accused, he proclaimed the faith with such presence of God that even his judges saw that he had the "face of an angel" (Acts 6:15). He suffered the stones in peace. So have thousands of others suffered and died under the hatred of men. But Christ suffered both the hatred of men *and the wrath of God* in his death. His heart and soul suffered the loss of God's friendship, even as his body was tortured. He endured the public humiliation throughout his life with the comfort that the Father was always with him. But not on the cross. There he suffered the loss of peace with God:

> . . . all my bones are out of joint;
> my heart is like wax;
> it is melted within my breast (Psalm 22:14).

I cannot quantify mathematically how Christ paid the complete punishment of all who would hope in him, but I see him paying it from the start, bearing our shame as well as our punishment.

5. The demand for faithfulness sounds to many in the modern church like a departure from the truth that salvation is the free gift of God. It sounds to them as if works of human effort rather than faith alone then becomes the basis of God's grace; and grace that is merited is no longer grace. While it is true that God's grace is free and unmerited, the New Testament does not see faithfulness as a work of human merit but rather as a consistent trust in God's meritorious work on our behalf. Faithfulness is *faith* exercising its dependence on and trust in God on a daily basis. Indeed, anything other than faithfulness is an expression of removing one's confidence in God and trusting in something else. That is why faithfulness is demanded throughout Scripture as the sign of faith that secures salvation. Jesus said, "You will be hated by all for my name's sake. *But the one who endures to the end will be saved*" (Mark 13:13). Second Timothy 2:12 says, "If *we endure*, we will also reign with him; if we deny him, he also will deny us." The condition for reigning with Christ is faithfulness to Christ. Therefore Hebrews 3:12-14 warns us, "Take care, brothers, lest there be in any of you an evil, unbelieving heart, leading you to fall away from the living God. But exhort one another every day, as long as it is called 'today,' that none of you may be hardened by the deceitfulness of sin. *For we share in Christ, if indeed we hold our original confidence firm to the end.*"

The necessity for persevering faith is a truth largely lost in the church today. In its place is a biblically truncated view that reduces faith to a one-time act of "believing" that is divorced from living a life of slowly maturing dependence and trust in God and his will. In some groups this truncated faith is then connected to all the promises of heaven so that, simply because at some point in their earlier life they made a "decision for Christ," even people who live with no passion for God and his glory are "assured of their eternal security" in spite of all the warnings of Scripture that "*if you live according to the flesh you will die*" (Romans 8:13). But Scripture sees saving faith as a *life-changing* gift of God. Through faith, God justifies (Romans 5:1), then sanctifies (2 Thessalonians 2:13), and eventually glorifies (Colossians 1:22-23) each recipient of his grace. Therefore enduring faith is necessary for salvation, and experiencing it is a sign of the enduring work of the grace of God, not human effort (Philippians 1:3-6; 1 Corinthians 1:8-9). Even Paul looked for this in himself as the basis for his hope for salvation (Philippians 3:10-11; 1 Corinthians 9:25-27; 2 Timothy 4:7).

God preserves his elect for all eternity *by giving them* a persevering faith. Therefore the necessity of faithfulness does not make faith any less a gift from God; rather, it defines the kind of faith that God gives us as his gift and helps us distinguish it from false forms of faith (see John 2:23-24; Matthew 13:21; James 2:14 for examples of people who had faith but not the kind that is saving in nature).

6. Archimedes, cited in Pappus of Alexandria, *Collection*, book 7, prop. 10, sec. 11.

CHAPTER 7: THE GREAT WORK EXPERIENCED

1. In contemporary psychology, there is a great emphasis on distinguishing between guilt and shame. When I do something bad I feel guilty. When I feel I *am* bad, that is shame. I do not follow this line of thinking. The premise that accompanies it is that shame is always misplaced. The therapist's goal is to persuade the patient that "you are not bad; what you did was bad." I do not think most people can hold the two separate except through a lot of mind games. What I do is a reflection of who I am. If I am doing bad, it is a sign that something is really wrong with *me*. The Bible teaches us that we are by nature sinners and that is why we sin. I use the terms *shame* and *guilt* to reflect a subtle difference rather than a big difference. Our feeling of guilt is more judicial, more the voice of conscience as an objective witness that we have done wrong. Shame is more the emotional pain we suffer because of our sin.

2. This is the lesson of Romans 5:3-4: "We rejoice in our sufferings, knowing that suffering produces endurance, and endurance produces character, and character produces hope." And James 1:2-4 says, "Count it all joy, my brothers, when you meet trials of various kinds, for you know that the testing of your faith produces steadfastness. And let steadfastness have its full effect, that you may be perfect and complete, lacking in nothing."

3. Some people use the term *limited atonement* to mean that Christ paid the full penalty for *some* people (those who believe). While this may be true, it confuses more than clarifies. I use the term *complete atonement* to put the emphasis where I think Scripture does, that Christ endured *all* the punishment of *all* who believe. God honors all who call to him in faith with complete forgiveness. "*Everyone* who calls upon the name of the Lord shall be saved" (Acts 2:21). See chapter 5, footnote 2 for more on this.

4. This is Daniel Fuller's translation of Romans 5:1. See Daniel Fuller, *The Unity of the Bible* (Grand Rapids, Mich.: Zondervan, 1992), 275.

5. Numbers 13–14 provides a clear example of how defiant and persistent unbelief can cloak itself in the humble language of repentance. God prepared Israel to take the Promised Land. Joshua and Caleb were ready to obey, but the rest were afraid and grumbled. In a sad way, God answered their prayers and refused to take them into the land. Instead they would live in the wilderness for forty years until they all died and the next generation would trust him for victory. "When Moses told these words to all the people of Israel, the people mourned greatly" (14:39). This certainly sounds like godly sorrow. They said, "We will go up to the place that the LORD has promised, for we have sinned" (14:40). This sounds like true repentance. But it was not. It was another example of continued defiance. They refused to humbly accept God's judgment on them. Moses said, "Why now are you transgressing the command of the LORD, when that will not succeed? Do not go up, for the Lord is not among you, lest you be struck down before your enemies" (14:41-42). They went up anyway, and were soundly defeated. God told them to go, and they said no. God told them not to go, and they said they would go anyway. Defiant unbelief *can* cloak itself in tears of regret. But where God's judgment is not yielded to as the best judgment, all else is defiance and unbelief, no matter how humble it sounds.

6. Second Corinthians 7:11 gives us a sense of the zeal with which habitual or addictive sins must be attacked if success is to be gained. It goes beyond feeling sorry. It is open warfare, moment by moment diligence, welcome accountability, constancy of prayer, fear and loathing, accepting the consequences (punishment), and more: "See what earnestness this godly grief has produced in you, but also what eagerness to clear yourselves, what indignation, what fear, what longing, what zeal, what punishment! At every point you have proved yourselves innocent in the matter."

7. Corrie ten Boom with Jamie Buckingham, *Tramp for the Lord* (Old Tappan, N.J.: Revell, 1974), 108.

CHAPTER 8: THE GREAT WORK ENJOYED

1. John Piper, *Desiring God* (Portland, Ore.: Multnomah, 1986), 41.

2. Some people suggest that it is a little mercenary to worship God for the good things he does for us. They direct us to love God and worship him for himself alone, and not for his benefits to us. There is a long tradition in the mystics that encourages this, but I am persuaded that it is wrong. I do concede that it sounds very spiritually mature. For example, Albert Day writes in his book *An Autobiography of Prayer,*
> We never really adore Him, until we arrive at the moment when we worship Him for what He is in Himself, apart from any consideration of the impact of His Divine Selfhood upon our desires and our welfare. Then we love Him for Himself alone. Then we adore Him, regardless of whether any personal benefit is in anticipation or not. . . . That is pure adoration. Nothing less is worthy of the name (cited in Bob Benson and Michael Benson, *Disciplines of the Inner Life* [Waco, Tex: Word, 1985], 53).

Just at the practical level, this advice demands a Herculean effort of mind control. I find it impossible to say, "I love You, God, You are so great!" without my mind recalling some of the great works God has done for *my* benefit. But more important, this advice is nowhere encouraged or demonstrated in the Bible. Instead, what we find are multiple examples that encourage us to love God *for his benefits.* Psalm 103:2 goes even further: "Bless the LORD, O my soul, and *forget not* all his benefits." Isaiah 61:10 calls to mind God's benefits as fuel for worship:
> I will greatly rejoice in the LORD;
> my soul shall exult in my God,
> *for* he has clothed me with the garments of salvation;
> he has covered me with the robe of righteousness

This is not mercenary. It is God-glorifying. Suppose my son came up to me and said, "Papa, I love you, but it is not because you feed me or teach me or play catch with me. I love you, but not because you ran me to the hospital when I got sick and came to my defense when that guy in the park tried to lure me into his car that day. I love you just because of who you are." I would not feel honored by this. I am his *father.* That is who I am. As his father, I am glorified in his dependence on me as a provider and protector. Let him praise me all he wants for the great things I have done for him. It will be good for him and it is proper for me. I am his father. So God is to be praised and glorified as our Father—our provider, the giver of good gifts. That is why the Bible does not encourage this sort of super-spirituality. God wants to show us his *goodness* (Exodus 33:19). That is how he desires to be praised.

3. Edward Taylor, "Should I with Silver Tools Delve Through the Hill," from *The Mentor Book of Major American Poets,* ed. Oscar Williams and Edwin Honig (New York: New American Library, 1962), 42.

4. Because of the deceitfulness of sin and our natural ability to deceive ourselves, we are called to examine ourselves to see whether or not we are in the faith (2 Corinthians 13:5; 2 Peter 1:10). We are to look for the *evidence* of saving faith, which is a heart glad to obey. We prove our status as children of God by the fruit of faithful obedience. See John 14:21; Romans 8:13; 1 Corinthians 6:9-11; Galatians 5:16-25; 1 John 1:5-7; 3:4-10.

5. Peter Kreeft, *Christianity for Modern Pagans* (San Francisco: Ignatius Press, 1993), 31.

CHAPTER 9: THE GREAT WORK SHARED

1. The phrase "finally obtaining the full measure of grace that brings eternal life" will be confusing and objectionable to some people. But the point I am trying to establish in this chapter is that forgiving others is *necessary* for final salvation. I am trying to be

faithful to Matthew 6:14-15, which says, "For if you forgive others their trespasses, your heavenly Father will also forgive you, but if you do not forgive others their trespasses, neither will your Father forgive your trespasses." This is a *conditional* promise of the grace of God and, as such, is largely confusing to the modern ear. John Piper is helpful here. He writes, "The biblical concept of unmerited, *conditional* grace is nearly unintelligible to many contemporary Christians who assume that *unconditionality* is the essence of all grace. To be sure, there is unconditional grace. And it is the glorious foundation of all else in the Christian life. But there is also *conditional* grace. For most people who breathe the popular air of grace and compassion today, *conditional* grace sounds like an oxymoron—like heavy feathers. So, for example, when, people hear the promise of James 4:6, that God 'gives grace *to the humble,*' many have a hard time thinking about a grace that is conditional upon humility" (John Piper, *Future Grace* [Sisters, Ore.: Multnomah, 1995], 11-12).

And yet, there are numerous examples of conditional grace in Scripture (see John 14:21; Luke 1:50; Hebrews 12:14; 1 John 1:7). The one we are owning up to in this chapter is the necessity of a forgiving heart. This does not mean we are meriting our salvation. Indeed, the *actions* that flow from a forgiving heart demonstrate that we have *faith* in God. How so? By forgiving, we actually demonstrate a *rejection* of human effort to bring about justice and vindication and show that we are trusting and depending on God's promise which says, "Vengeance is mine, I will repay" (Romans 12:19; see also Deuteronomy 32:35). That is why God can require us to forgive those who have victimized us—because forgiveness is *faith in God* expressing itself—and this faith is what connects us to the gift of grace and eternal life.

I understand all the conditions of grace this way, as various expressions of faith in God. The love for God required in John 14:21 is the work of God's grace according to Deuteronomy 30:6. Obedience to the will of God is one of the conditions of grace (Matthew 7:21), but it is also an expression of faith in the sanctifying power of God (Philippians 2:13). Even the condition of "doing good" (Romans 2:7, NIV) is really an expression of faith according to James 2:14-19. As James said, "Show me your faith apart from your works, and I will show you my faith *by my works*" (2:18).

Therefore, I think Piper is right to help us see that,
Conditional grace is not earned grace. It is not merited. "Earned grace" is an oxymoron. Grace cannot be earned. The very meaning of grace is that the one receiving grace does not deserve it—has not earned it. If a philanthropist pays $80,000 for your college education on the condition that you graduate from high school, you have not earned the gift but you have met a condition. It is possible to meet a condition for receiving grace and yet not earn grace. Conditional grace does not mean earned grace. How can this be?
The part of this answer that needs to be said here is that when God's grace is based on a condition, that condition is also a work of God's grace. This guarantees the absolute freeness of grace. The philanthropist mentioned above may even become the personal tutor for a failing high school student to insure that he does get his diploma and so meets the condition for the $80,000 grant (Piper, *Future Grace,* 78-79).

In regard to the need to forgive others, God not only demands it, he works in our heart to help us meet the condition of forgiving others. He tutors us about the idolatry of passing judgment as if we were God rather than a child of God. He teaches us how to respond and then empowers us to that end, as this chapter shows.
2. For full treatment of Fuller's analogy see Daniel P. Fuller, *Gospel and Law* (Grand Rapids, Mich.: Eerdmans, 1980), 117-120.
3. Often attributed to Thomas Adams (1612–1653).
4. The condition is really one of faith. Forgiving others is one way in which saving faith expresses its confidence in God. For example, if I say, "I have talent!" your immediate question will be, "How does this talent reveal itself? What do you do that shows you have talent?" If I say, "I just have it inside me," you will consider it a very strange

claim. In the same way, James argues, "Show me your faith apart from your works, and I will show you my faith by my works" (James 2:18). Forgiving others is one of the talents of saving faith. It shows we are trusting in God's promise of Romans 12:19: "Vengeance is mine, I will repay."

5. Gary Thomas, "A Proper Double Standard," *World,* February 3, 1996, 26.

6. Corrie ten Boom with Jamie Buckingham, *Tramp for the Lord* (Old Tappan, N.J.: Revell, 1974), 56-57.

7. Heather Gemmen, *Startling Beauty* (Colorado Springs: Cook, 2004), 172.

8. Ibid., 14-15, emphasis in source.

9. Ibid., 224.

10. Cited in *National and International Religion Report,* March 6, 1995.

CHAPTER 10: THE GREAT WORK UNSHEATHED

1. See Nathan Cobb, "Ray Hammond's Sacrifice," *Boston Globe,* June 6, 1996, 33.

2. Charles Swindoll, *Improving Your Serve: The Art of Unselfish Living* (Waco, Tex.: Word, 1981).

3. Dietrich Bonhoeffer, *Letters and Papers from Prison* (New York: Macmillan, 1953), 136.

4. God told Abraham that his Great Work consisted of all the *peoples* of the earth being blessed. Jesus commissioned us to take the blessing to *all nations* in fulfillment of the Abrahamic promise. There is broad agreement that this does not mean the sovereign countries. The growing consensus is that God has in mind the distinct cultural groups within each country. For example, Nigeria is a sovereign nation, but it has 490 ethnic groups. There are 470 languages in Nigeria, though 21 major languages are spoken by 96 percent of the population. There are three major zones in Nigeria containing 36 states (from Patrick Johnstone and Jason Mandryk, *Operation World, Twenty-first Century Edition* [Waynesboro, Ga.: Paternoster USA, 2001]). In 1982, a meeting in Lausanne, Switzerland, was held by missions experts to clarify what a people group was and whether the blessing of the gospel had reached people groups to the degree that fulfilled the promise of God. While humbly acknowledging that they do not know for sure, they agreed on some working definitions. A people group "is a significantly large grouping of individuals who perceive themselves to have a common affinity for one another because of their shared language, religion, ethnicity, residence, occupation, class or caste, situation, etc. Or a combination of these." For evangelistic purposes it is "the largest group within which the Gospel can spread as a church planting movement without encountering barriers of understanding or acceptance." They also agreed upon a working definition of an unreached people group: "A group within which there is no indigenous community of believing Christians able to evangelize this people group" (see Ralph Winter, "Unreached Peoples: Recent Developments in the Concept," *Mission Frontiers,* August–September 1989, 12).

5. These numbers come from a *Mission Frontiers* chart developed from the research data of the Lausanne Statistics Task Force and their chairman, David Barrett, author of the *World Christian Encyclopedia.* The estimates reflect the number of "serious Christian believers" only, and do not include nominal or cultural identifications of Christianity. See *Mission Frontiers,* January–February 1996, 5.

6. Ralph Winter, "The Diminishing Task," *Mission Frontiers,* June–August 1991, 53.

7. This number comes from David Barrett, editor of the *World Christian Encyclopedia,* and from the Lausanne Statistics Task Force. The estimates reflect the number of "serious Christian believers" only, and do not include nominal or cultural identifications of Christianity. Cited in *Mission Frontiers,* May–June 1993, 6.

8. Herbert Schlossberg, *Called to Suffer, Called to Triumph* (Portland, Ore.: Multnomah, 1990), 43-44.

9. Earle E. Cairns, *An Endless Line of Splendor* (Wheaton, Ill.: Tyndale, 1986).

10. To understand how people living for the glory of God have shaped our modern culture, see Rodney Stark, *For the Glory of God: How Monotheism Led to Reformations, Science, Witch-hunts, and the End of Slavery* (Princeton, N.J.: Princeton University Press, 2003).

11. Ralph Waldo Emerson, "Give All to Love," in *The Mentor Book of Major American Poets,* ed. Oscar Williams and Edwin Honig (New York: New American Library, 1962), 61.

12. Ralph Winter, "World Evangelization by 2000 A.D.—Is It Possible?" USCWM Series 05-296 (Pasadena, Calif.: William Carey Library, 1996), 1.

13. Robertson McQuilkin, "Living by Vows," *Christianity Today,* October 8, 1990, 40.

GENERAL INDEX

SCRIPTURE INDEX

1 Thessalonians
1:3   166
4:11-12   133
4:13   64

2 Thessalonians
2:13   115, 125
3:14-15   117

1 Timothy
1:15-16   39
2:12   177-178n4
4:2   144

2 Timothy
1:9   85
2:25   14

Titus
2:11-12   13, 125
2:14   13, 160

Hebrews
2:2   95
3:12-14   177-178n4
4:16   110
9:14   109, 115, 159
10:22   107, 110
10:26-29   116
10:35   116
11:32   167
11:37   167
12:2   109, 118, 130
12:7   119
12:10-11   119
12:29   58

James
1:2-4   179n2
1:9   176n3
1:11   176n3
1:16-17   50
2:13   154
2:14-19   180-181n1
2:18 180-181n1, 181-182n4
2:19   103
4:6   59, 180-181n1
5:1   176n3
5:2   176n3
5:5   176n3

1 Peter
1:2   115
1:3   127

1:7   128
2:23   140
3:18   115
3:21   111
4:11   161-162
5:2   159

2 Peter
1:10   128
2:17   100

1 John
1:9   98
1:10   42
2:3   14
2:4   127
3:6   127
3:9   126
3:19-20   110
3:21-22   110
4:10   97

Jude
13   56
24   15

Revelation
1:14   58
7:9-10   164
11:17-18   60
14:19-20   56
19:2   60
19:7   124
20:15   60
21:4   13